FREE Study Skills DVD Offer

Dear Customer,

Thank you for your purchase from Mometrix! We consider it an honor and privilege that you have purchased our product and want to ensure your satisfaction.

As a way of showing our appreciation and to help us better serve you, we have developed a Study Skills DVD that we would like to give you for <u>FREE</u>. **This DVD covers our "best practices" for studying for your exam, from using our study materials to preparing for the day of the test.**

All that we ask is that you email us your feedback that would describe your experience so far with our product. Good, bad or indifferent, we want to know what you think!

To get your **FREE Study Skills DVD**, email <u>freedvd@mometrix.com</u> with "FREE STUDY SKILLS DVD" in the subject line and the following information in the body of the email:

   a. The name of the product you purchased.

   b. Your product rating on a scale of 1-5, with 5 being the highest rating.

   c. Your feedback. It can be long, short, or anything in-between, just your impressions and experience so far with our product. Good feedback might include how our study material met your needs and will highlight features of the product that you found helpful.

   d. Your full name and shipping address where you would like us to send your free DVD.

If you have any questions or concerns, please don't hesitate to contact me directly.

Thanks again!

Sincerely,

Jay Willis
Vice President
<u>jay.willis@mometrix.com</u>
1-800-673-8175

TABLE OF CONTENTS

Top 20 Test Taking Tips

1. Carefully follow all the test registration procedures
2. Know the test directions, duration, topics, question types, how many questions
3. Setup a flexible study schedule at least 3-4 weeks before test day
4. Study during the time of day you are most alert, relaxed, and stress free
5. Maximize your learning style; visual learner use visual study aids, auditory learner use auditory study aids
6. Focus on your weakest knowledge base
7. Find a study partner to review with and help clarify questions
8. Practice, practice, practice
9. Get a good night's sleep; don't try to cram the night before the test
10. Eat a well balanced meal
11. Know the exact physical location of the testing site; drive the route to the site prior to test day
12. Bring a set of ear plugs; the testing center could be noisy
13. Wear comfortable, loose fitting, layered clothing to the testing center; prepare for it to be either cold or hot during the test
14. Bring at least 2 current forms of ID to the testing center
15. Arrive to the test early; be prepared to wait and be patient
16. Eliminate the obviously wrong answer choices, then guess the first remaining choice
17. Pace yourself; don't rush, but keep working and move on if you get stuck
18. Maintain a positive attitude even if the test is going poorly
19. Keep your first answer unless you are positive it is wrong
20. Check your work, don't make a careless mistake

Nature and Needs of Gifted and Talented Students

Gifted Children

Former U. S. Commissioner of Education Sidney P. Marland, Jr., in his August 1971 report to Congress, stated, "Gifted and talented children are those identified by professionally qualified persons who by virtue of outstanding abilities are capable of high performance. These are children who require differentiated educational programs and/or services beyond those normally provided by the regular school program in order to realize their contribution to self and society". The same report continued: "Children capable of high performance include those with demonstrated achievement and/or potential ability in any of the following areas, singly or in combination:

- General intellectual ability
  Specific academic aptitude
  Creative or productive thinking
  Leadership ability
  Visual or performing arts
  Psychomotor ability

Characteristics of a gifted student

- Shows superior reasoning powers and marked ability to handle ideas; can generalize readily from specific facts and can see subtle relationships; has outstanding problem-solving ability.
- Shows persistent intellectual curiosity; asks searching questions; shows exceptional interest in the nature of man and the universe.
- Is markedly superior in quality and quantity of written or spoken vocabulary; is interested in the subtleties of words and their uses.
- Reads avidly and absorbs books well beyond his or her years.
- Learns quickly and easily and retains what is learned; recalls important details, concepts and principles; comprehends readily.
- Shows insight into arithmetical problems that require careful reasoning and grasps mathematical concepts readily.
- Shows creative ability or imaginative expression in such things as music, art, dance, drama; shows finesse in bodily control.
- Sustains concentration for lengthy periods and shows outstanding responsibility and independence in classroom work.
- Sets realistically high standards for self; is self-critical in evaluation. Shows initiative and originality in intellectual work; shows flexibility in thinking and considers problems from a number of viewpoints.
- Observes keenly and is responsive to new ideas.
- Shows social poise and a mature ability to communicate with adults.
- Gets excitement and pleasure from intellectual challenge.

Giftedness

Educators and advocates agree that no universal consensus exists regarding the definition of giftedness. The National Association for Gifted Children (NAGC) asserts that the concept of giftedness, like the concepts of intelligence and talent, is fluid in nature. Depending upon culture and other contexts, such concepts can be manifested and perceived differently. Moreover, the term "gifted" has a variety of meanings and subtleties within each meaning, even in school systems and within individual schools. In any given school, individual educators likely hold a range of different personal beliefs regarding this term. The NAGC finds that individuals showing "...aptitude (...exceptional ability to reason and learn) or competence (documented performance or achievement in top 10% or rarer) in one or more domains" (2008) are gifted. They define domains as structured activity areas within symbol systems such as language, math, or music, and/or within sensorimotor skill sets such as art, dance, or sports.

While America has federal laws governing special education services for students with disabilities, these laws do not contain specific provisions that mandate each state to offer special education services for gifted and talented students. As a result, each American state can create its own definitions of giftedness and talent and its own programs for gifted and talented students. A state's definition will inform how it identifies such students; how it decides eligibility for services; and the kinds of educational programs it develops. Indiana, Nebraska, and Washington use the term "high ability student." Eighteen states use "gifted," while the other twenty-five states use "gifted and talented." Four states—Massachusetts, Minnesota, New Hampshire, and South Dakota—have no state definition of giftedness or talent. Giftedness and talent are defined by the state legislatures in 25 states, while the remaining 21 states have each mandated or authorized their state Boards of Education to define these terms.

Giftedness vs. talent

Canadian psychology professor/researcher Dr. Francoys Gagné (not to be confused with American educational psychologist Dr. Robert M. Gagné), in his "A Differentiated Model of Giftedness and Talent (DMGT)" (1985, updated 2000), clearly distinguishes giftedness from talent using the criteria of competence/ability/aptitude versus performance/skill/achievement. He finds that "...superior natural abilities (called aptitudes or gifts), in at least one ability domain..." that constitute giftedness are "untrained and spontaneously expressed." He defines talent as "...superior mastery of systematically developed abilities (or skills) and knowledge in at least one field of human activity..." The differences are (1) that talent requires methodical development and learning, while giftedness needs no training; and (2) that gifts are in "ability domains" while talents are in "fields of human activity." He designates both as placing an individual in the top 10% of age peers in a given domain or field. His ability/aptitude domains include Intellectual, Creative, Socioaffective, and Sensorimotor.

Demonstrating gifted behavior

Dr. Joseph Renzulli and colleague Dr. Sally Reis, both from the University of Connecticut, created a Schoolwide Enrichment Model (SEM) (1976, 1977, 1985, 1997) for academically gifted and talented students and for all schools to develop students' strengths and talents. Renzulli focuses more, as do other behaviorists, on students' actions—i.e. gifted behavior—than on students' abilities/potentials. He proposes that three groups of characteristics must interact to produce gifted behavior: (1) above average abilities, either general or specific; (2) high levels of motivation; and (3) high levels of creativity. He identifies any child who succeeds either in having or in developing this combination of characteristics and applying it to any "potentially valuable" field of human activity as gifted or talented. Renzulli states in the SEM that gifted behaviors exist "in certain people (not all people), at certain times (not all the time), and under certain circumstances (not all circumstances)."

- 6 -

Domains of aptitude (identified by F. Gagné) are Intellectual, Creative, Socioaffective, Sensorimotor, and "others." A student who is gifted in the Intellectual domain might demonstrate this giftedness through superior learning, academic and/or otherwise, as evidenced by extent, breadth, depth of knowledge and/or speed and ease of learning; through superior achievement in school grades and standardized tests; and/or facility beyond grade level in reading or mathematics, etc. Gifts in the Creative domain might be demonstrated by advanced learning and understanding of principles in music, art, etc.; superior musical interpretation, performance, and/or composition; superior composition and execution in visual arts; originating mathematical/scientific formulas; or producing inventions. Socioaffective gifts might appear in a student's heightened ability in making friends, helping peers resolve conflicts, disarming bullies/hostility, and empathy for others. Sensorimotor gifts can emerge in athletic abilities or physical abilities for certain crafts and arts. "Others" includes extra-sensory perceptions such as precognition, clairvoyance, and communicating with spiritual realms.

Individual and group differences among gifted children

Researchers have pointed out that such individual factors as genetic composition, life experiences, personality, and personal development, as well as the influences of families, interpersonal relationships, and educational experiences result in individual variations in the ways in which gifted children respond to and express their special abilities. While the research has acknowledged individual differences among gifted children for at least 50 years, less work has been done to identify various groups among the gifted. Roeper (1982) theorized five types of gifted children based on their approaches for coping with and expressing their feelings. These types include: (1) the Perfectionist; (2) the Child/Adult; (3) the Winner of the Competition; (4) the Self-Critic; and (5) the Well-Integrated Child. Betts and Neihart (1988) identified six "profiles" of gifted students based on their needs, feelings, and behaviors: (I) The Successful; (II) The Challenging; (III) The Underground; (IV) The Dropouts; (V) The Double-Labeled; and (VI) The Autonomous Learner.

Types of gifted students

Challenging

Gifted students described as "challenging" are "divergently gifted." In other words, they are highly creative and unconventional. Schools often do not identify such students for gifted programs unless such programs have been implemented for a sufficient number of years and teachers have received enough in-service training. These children do not learn to use the system to their own benefit as more "successful" gifted students do. They tend to question authority and challenge teachers in class. Consequently, they are rarely rewarded for their abilities and often experience conflict. Those children who challenge their peers are not accepted, while others are liked for their originality and humor. They can be disruptive in class due to their spontaneous behaviors. Frustration and low self-esteem are risks for these students. Additionally, they may risk delinquency, drug use, and dropping out of high school if they do not receive suitable intervention by the time they reach middle school/junior high school.

Dropout

Researchers identify a salient characteristic of the "dropout" gifted student as anger. These students have experienced long-term failure of the system to meet their needs. Disappointment with themselves and

- 7 -

with adults along with their feelings of rejection can lead to depression. In these students, this depression may manifest as social withdrawal or as defensive acting-out behavior. These students often have abilities and interests in unusual areas not included in school curricula, so they are not affirmed or rewarded for these abilities and interests. School may seem irrelevant or even antagonistic to those students with very different gifts. Many dropout students were not identified as gifted until later, e.g. in high school. This long-term lack of recognition and appropriate educational programming engenders resentment, bitterness, and low self-esteem. Educational experts recommend that these students need individual and group counseling, a close working relationship with a trusted adult, and diagnostic testing for possible remedial areas. Experts also state that traditional programming is not indicated for "dropout" gifted students.

Successful

Researchers have estimated that about 90 percent of students identified as gifted fit the profile described as "successful." These children are most often identified as gifted because they have learned which behaviors adults prefer; as a result of this learning, these children demonstrate the adults' preferred behaviors. . They typically achieve high scores on IQ, aptitude, and achievement tests. They are not likely to display problem behaviors because they crave adults' approval of and know which behaviors will obtain this desired result. Although many people expect such children to succeed independently, such success is often not the case. The researchers find these children tend to depend on adults for direction. Bored with regular curriculum, these children often "work the system" in order to achieve with minimal effort, not developing the autonomy necessary to pursue their own interests and gifts. Liked by peers and rewarded by adults,

these students grow up socially well-adjusted but not prepared for life's changing demands; as adults, they may be underachievers.

Underground

Commonly researchers have found that middle school females often make up a group of students classified as the "underground" type of gifted student. In pre-adolescence and early adolescence, girls' need for group belonging and peer acceptance increases exponentially; as a result, many girls will hide their gifts or deny them to fit into a group. The researchers note that gifted boys in this category tend to go underground later, typically in high school, as a reaction to the pressure to join athletic teams and events and to their desire for identification with more popular "jocks" rather than less popular "nerds." Anxious and insecure, "underground" students have needs that conflict with adult expectations. Adult pressure only worsens their denial and resistance. Experts find that they benefit more from acceptance. As such, experts advise adults neither to push nor to permit abandonment of all prior interests in order to fit in; instead, adults should help these students find alternatives to meet their academic needs during what is considered a period of transition.

Double-labeled

Researchers identify "double-labeled" gifted students as those with both giftedness and physical, emotional, or learning disabilities. Although dual diagnosis is possible with thorough evaluation, most educational programs for the gifted neither identify such students nor afford them differentiated instructional programming that integrates and meets their specialized needs. Because of their combinations of gifts with disabilities, schools can frequently overlook these students, as many of them display behaviors that school personnel do not associate with giftedness. Students with learning disabilities can display poor organizational skills, problems with memory, difficulties with reading, poor handwriting, and etc. Those students with emotional or behavior disorders may exhibit disruptive behavior. Due to the contradictions of their abilities and disabilities, these students are often confused and stressed and suffer from low self-esteem. Often these students are either perceived as average and therefore ignored, or targeted for remediation of their disabilities while their respective gifts are overlooked.

Autonomous learner

Educational researchers find that parents may observe "autonomous learner" types of gifted children exhibiting signs of this style at home, but these children typically demonstrate it somewhat later in school once they have learned the system. Unlike the "successful" type of gifted student, who seems to have high self-esteem but depends on adult direction and reinforcement, autonomous learners have strong internalized self-concepts. Rather than meeting the system's demands with as little work as possible as do "successful" gifted students, autonomous gifted learners employ the system to create new opportunities to meet their own needs. Self-directed and independent, these students are characterized by self-acceptance and risk-taking ability. They feel secure about forming personal and educational goals. They exhibit a strong sense of self-efficacy (belief in their ability to do things) and personal power. They are active rather than passive, and they express their needs, emotions, and goals with freedom, but also within appropriate limits.

Uneven development

Educational researchers have found that intellectually gifted children do not always develop evenly across all domains of ability. While some gifted students excel in all areas, particularly in the higher grades, many more of these students demonstrate comparatively greater gifts in certain domains than in others. One example of uneven development very common among younger gifted children occurs when their cognitive and conceptual abilities develop far in advance of their physical motor skills. When this uneven development happens, while a young child is capable of more sophisticated ideation, he or she is incapable of executing his or her ideas physically due to less advanced motor abilities. This frustrating inequity proves frustrating and produces tantrums in many children. Another example of uneven development occurs when an intellectually gifted child uses his or her superior cognitive skills to interact with the environment almost exclusively, leaving his or her emotional and social skills underdeveloped from lack of practice.

Strengths and "problem" behavior

Intellectually gifted students often have advanced organizational skills. This advancement benefits them academically, since it facilitates learning. However, this advancement also can manifest in these students exhibiting a need to organize things and people beyond their own academic subjects. Positively, this characteristic contributes to leadership qualities; negatively, it contributes to making rules too complex for others and to being perceived as bossy. Intellectually gifted students often possess knowledge ahead of their peers in both level and breadth; they frequently have larger vocabularies and more facile use of their respective vocabularies. Problems associated with these strengths include boredom with school and classmates and the potential for using language to manipulate others. Intellectually gifted students tend to have high expectations both for themselves and others. While this strength is a motivational quality, its drawbacks include perfectionism, a lack of tolerance for their own and/or others' shortcomings, and a potential for developing depression due to disappointment over unmet expectations.

Intellectually gifted students often learn and remember new information more quickly than other students. A potential side effect of this facility involves impatience with other less gifted, as well as with routine procedures they find superfluous and limiting. The curious/inquisitive nature of intellectually gifted students as well as their need to seek meaning can result in questions that embarrass others; others' perceptions that the gifted students are nosy and/or rude; and perceptions that the gifted students go overboard in pursuing their interests. Another strength involves internalized motivation; however, as a downside, these students can seem overly willful and resistant to direction from others. Students with superior capacities for synthesis and conceptualization tend to enjoy solving problems and dealing with abstract ideas. However, these students are more likely to question/challenge teaching practices and routines. They also tend to focus on truth and fairness, so they may have excessive humanitarian worries and/or difficulty accepting inequitable realities in life.

Often intellectually gifted students are sensitive and promote empathy for others. The problem associated with this area of giftedness involves the students' need for the acceptance of others, as well as an accompanying oversensitivity to rejection and/or criticism. Creative and inventive students enjoy finding new ways to do things. This gift proves a boon to society in terms of innovation, but it also can be perceived as disruptive and

abnormal. Intellectually gifted students often have longer attention spans than other students, can concentrate on one subject more intensively, and are more persistent in the areas interesting them. Many important accomplishments are attributable to these qualities. However, these qualities also can result in the neglect of other academic subjects and/or persons and relationships, ignoring interruptions, and being thought stubborn. Many intellectually gifted students are highly alert, enthusiastic, and eager to learn; in addition, these students may possess high energy levels. These assets can be misperceived as hyperactivity/overactivity. These students can also become frustrated when inactive.

Many intellectually gifted students are academically independent. Superior abilities for learning, knowing, and understanding afford them both the skills and the confidence for autonomy and self-direction in learning. These skills and confidence, plus their thinking and learning differently from their age peers, promote self-reliance in such students. They are likely to prefer individualized tasks. Because of these factors, these students may be seen by others as not conforming to accepted norms. They also may reject input from their peers, teachers, or parents, and these other individuals likely will not receive such rejection well. Greater amounts of versatility and diversity in their abilities and interests give these students more options, but these characteristics also can cause time-management issues and cause a disorganized impression. Strong senses of humor can be misconstrued by age peers, and as a result these students may evolve into "class clowns." Their tendencies to seek causal relationships can make them uncomfortable with irrational/illogical feelings or traditions.

Dual exceptionalities

Gifted students with disabling conditions remain a major group of underserved and under-stimulated youth. The focus on accommodations for their disabilities may preclude the recognition and development of their cognitive abilities. It is not unexpected, then, to find a significant discrepancy between the measured academic potential of these students and their actual performance in the classroom. In order for these children to reach their potential, it is imperative that their intellectual strengths be recognized and nurtured, at the same time as their disability is accommodated appropriately.

Needs that instructional curriculum design and delivery must address

Some qualities that educators have found intellectually gifted students to exhibit include curiosity and an inquisitive nature (i.e. wanting to find out and know things, to understand processes, and to answer questions); complexity in their thinking, personality, and behavior; possessing an extraordinary capacity for learning; more diversity among their interests in learning; a preference for learning subjects holistically rather than in parts or analytically; a tendency to learn more intuitively than methodically or logically; tendencies toward perfectionism; and a corresponding tendency to exhibit fear regarding risk-taking. Intellectually gifted students also demonstrate the need to reflect on their own thinking and learning (self-reflection); the need to achieve an understanding and an acceptance of the nature of giftedness; a need to develop healthy and positive skills for social interactions and relationships; and a need to solve problems in real life as a way to find meaning and connections in life.

Fluency, flexibility, originality, and elaboration

Fluency, flexibility, originality, and elaboration are four qualities considered by many experts as key components of creativity. The original version of Torrance's creativity scales measured these four qualities. Fluency refers to an individual's ability to generate a large number of concepts or of alternate solutions to a problem. Flexibility refers to an individual's ability to approach a problem from a variety of perspectives, therefore enabling the individual to come up with ideas and solutions to problems in a variety of categories. Originality refers to an individual's ability to generate unique or uncommon ideas. Fluency, flexibility, and originality are hallmarks of creative thinking. These qualities also are reflected in divergent thinking, a key characteristic of creativity involving generating many different possibilities rather than narrowing ideas down to one conclusion, as in convergent thinking. Elaboration in creative thinking involves the ability to add details to embellish one's ideas or results.

Emotional characteristics

Gifted children often display emotional intensity by experiencing and expressing extremes of emotions. They likely exhibit more emotional sensitivity than other children. They may feel more anxiety, guilt, and sense of responsibility than other children their age. Despite their superior abilities, they can feel inadequate or inferior due to their extreme sensitivity, high standards, perfectionism, and tendency to internalize. They may be shy and timid, and as a result they may be lonely. However, they are also likely to show concern for other people. Their sense of right and wrong is often heightened, prompting strong reactions against dishonesty, hypocrisy, and injustices.

They tend to retain stronger memories of emotional experiences. They may have difficulty adjusting to changes. Because of their emotional sensitivity, they are susceptible to depression. They tend to have a need for security. They may suffer from physiological symptoms of emotional states, such as getting a stomach ache from feeling anxious.

Convergent thinking vs. divergent thinking

Convergent and divergent are opposites. In convergent thinking, different thoughts narrow/come together (converge) on one conclusion. An example is forensic detective work. If a suspect's fingerprints are found on the murder weapon, his DNA is found on the victim, and eyewitnesses place him at the scene of the crime at the time of death, then these pieces of evidence converge to show that suspect's guilt. Considering whether this suspect was framed or whether the evidence was circumstantial would involve some divergent thinking in which different thoughts proliferate/separate (diverge) into many possibilities. Some creativity tests ask test takers to generate as many different uses as possible for a brick, tin can, paper clip, etc. Listing all the things you can build with a brick is not considered an instance of divergent thinking, because building is one category. Holding papers/cloths/leaves together with paper clips is convergent; using paper clips as snowshoes for mice is divergent.

Characteristics of intellectually gifted children

Social
Because intellectually gifted students are proficient in understanding abstract concepts, they often show an interest in social and philosophical issues. They are typically concerned about seeing justice done and tend to object to actions or decisions they perceive as unfair. Developmental psychologists such as Jean Piaget and Lawrence Kohlberg would say that such children display advanced moral reasoning. Because they have high standards for themselves and others as well as the ability to do many things better than others, even achieving perfection in certain tasks, they tend to be perfectionists. They often have more internal motivation than external motivation to achieve. Desires such as wanting good grades and teacher approval are external, whereas desires such as wanting to learn about a subject or to beat one's own personal best on tests are internal. Other prevalent characteristics include: good relational skills with parents, teachers, and age peers; well-developed senses of humor; energetic approaches; and emotional and physical sensitivity.

Aesthetic
The Polish psychiatrist and psychologist Kasimierz Dabrowski (1902-1980) proposed intensities he termed "overexcitabilities" or "supersensitivities" in gifted children. His concept of sensual intensity involves heightened awareness and perception of the senses of vision, hearing, touch, smell, and taste. Gifted toddlers with this sensitivity may hate the feel of grass on their bare feet, gifted children may feel nauseated at the smells of certain foods, and/or they may overeat other foods that taste especially good to them. This characteristic is consistent with a craving for pleasure and a need or desire for comfort, two additional characteristics of gifted children with sensory sensitivities. These children often are more sensitive to air pollution and/or to the discomfort of labels/tags in clothing. Another aspect of this sensitivity involves the aesthetic appreciation of beautiful jewelry, visual art, music, literature, and the beauties of nature. Children with this sensitivity often can be moved to tears by beauty.

Imagination

Dabrowski identified the following sensitivities gifted children: psychomotor, sensual, emotional, intellectual, and imaginational. Many gifted children have very vivid imaginations. They are likely to have vivid dreams and to recall them. Because their imaginations allow them to conceive of diverse possibilities, to see things from different viewpoints, to look at things in new/different ways, to be inventive, and to generate original and unusual ideas, these children are likely to develop and utilize good senses of humor. They also are likely to daydream and have imaginary friends. They tend to love fantasy, poetry, drama, and music. They are more likely to have strong visualization skills as well as mental images with more detail than the mental images of other children. Because they can imagine all sorts of possibilities, they can envision the worst case scenarios for any situation. This characteristic can promote fear of the unknown, of taking risks, and of new situations.

Underachievement

Some gifted students express their gifts during the earlier parts of their childhood by pursuing areas of special interest to them, excelling in certain school subjects, and working on advanced projects. Some students suddenly drop all these activities, deny their previous interests, or claim they have lost interest or outgrown them. Experts have found girls most likely to exhibit this trend during middle school/junior high school, while boys are more likely exhibit this trend in high school. Researchers attribute the change to social and emotional needs, especially in school. Girls approaching and entering adolescence experience a great increase in their needs for peer acceptance and for a sense of belonging. Consequently, some gifted girls will hide or deny their giftedness in order to fit in with a non-gifted group of peers. Boys in high school often experience pressure to play sports, a celebrated skill, while academic excellence without athleticism is ridiculed.

Not identified as gifted earlier in school, some gifted students reach their high school years without any special educational interventions or programs designed for their unique abilities. These students may have been overlooked in the school system if their gifts exist outside of their schools' areas of curricula. While these gifted students may have the ability to perform well in certain subjects, teachers might find these students' different methods of achieving such performances unacceptable or invalid. Furthermore, such students may attend a school in which personnel lack sufficient training or experience with giftedness. By the time students receive neither acknowledgement nor support for their gifts in high school, they have felt rejected for years and are usually angry and/or depressed. Without support or appropriate curriculum they will not achieve and may drop out of school.

Some gifted students figure out early on which behaviors are desired and rewarded by adults, and then these students use their superior abilities to produce these behaviors. They are successful according to adult standards and appear to have high self-esteem because of the adult reinforcement they receive. They are not identified with behavior problems because they comply with adults' wishes in order to succeed. However, such students, especially when placed in regular classes with mainstream curricula, often secretly feel bored with school. These students use their expertise to get through school by expending the minimal effort possible. As a result, they do not develop the independence and skills needed for self-direction, nor do they explore subjects of personal interest to them. Instead, they rely on adults for direction, guidance, and feedback. They often develop into adults who display competence but not originality or imagination. When they continue these behaviors in adulthood, they can become underachievers in relation to their ability.

Some gifted students have superior abilities that they can express congruently within the traditionally accepted framework of academic performance and achievement. Other gifted students have superior abilities best expressed outside of this framework. These students often think in more markedly different ways than other students, who often fail to understand them. They may also have talents not included in school curricula. They do not receive rewards for their gifts in the same manner as students with more traditionally acceptable gifts. As a result, the gifted students become frustrated. Due to the unconventional nature of these students' gifts, educators often do not identify them as gifted, so they receive little instructional support. They also are often highly creative. Their spontaneity can be perceived as disruptive in school. With their self-esteem compromised and their gifts not nurtured, such students likely underachieve in school and exhibit increased risk for dropout if they do not receive specialized instructional attention.

Co-existing disability

Some gifted students also have a co-existing physical, emotional, psychiatric, behavioral, or learning disability. This co-existing occurrence of giftedness and disability complicates diagnosis. For example, intellectually gifted children can exhibit a number of behaviors that appear very similar to the behaviors of children with attention deficit hyperactivity disorder (behaviors such as high energy and activity levels, impulsive actions, rapid speech, etc.). They may exhibit

compulsive organizing and possible obsessive-compulsive disorder. Most educational programs for gifted students do not address concomitant disabilities, while conversely most programs for disabled students do not address giftedness. Researchers are endeavoring to remedy these errors. At times teachers might overlook these students' areas of giftedness and instead focus on the behaviors produced by the students' disabilities. Teachers may not consider that a child with messy handwriting or disruptive classroom behavior, for example, might exhibit giftedness in areas such as art, science, music, dance, or athletics.

Environmental factors

The influence of environmental variables can be seen historically through creative proliferation at certain times and places. For example, Florence, Italy in the 15th century; the Harlem Renaissance in 1920s and 1930s New York in America; and San Francisco, California in 1960s America all exhibited unusual amounts of creative inspiration and production. Some of the environmental factors that allow people with creative gifts to express them in meaningful and socially valuable ways include: social support for a subculture consisting of creative persons; availability and accessibility of materials and resources for creative production; a political and cultural climate that allows freedom of expression; and the existence of patrons with the means and interest to lend financial, material, and moral support to creative endeavors. Influences impeding creative expression include the race, gender, and socioeconomic status of some gifted individuals due to others' stereotyping and lowered expectations because of such environmental characteristics.

Nurturing giftedness

Teachers can observe student behaviors in order to identify their personal interests and abilities. When they notice a student excelling in a certain subject area, teachers can provide enrichment activities for that student. Even in a general education classroom with no gifted programs, teachers can provide additional activities in preferred areas to students who show evidence of giftedness by asking for additional activities. Teachers can vary their instruction by offering activities and assignments at higher grade levels to gifted students not challenged or even bored at their class' grade level. Teachers pressed for time can arrange peer tutoring by older and/or more advanced students to allow younger gifted students more 1:1 interaction and individualized learning at the students' own pace. Teachers can help gifted students plan and develop special projects in their areas of interest, allowing them to learn about these areas in more depth and with more complexity.

Parents can begin reading to children regularly as soon as the children are able to attend. Furthermore, as children develop, parents can encourage children to read to them as well. As children grow, parents can observe and encourage their interests/aptitudes. Providing books for verbally precocious children is crucial (libraries offer a good option if funds are limited), since good writers begin as good readers. Parents can give children with mathematical talents numerical puzzles and games. For children interested in producing reactions by mixing substances, junior chemistry sets or household materials can be provided. Beginner telescopes and trips to the local planetarium are good for children fascinated with stars and planets. Parents can provide interested children with introductory geology sample sets and take them on local field trips to discover rocks, minerals, and/or fossils. Basic art supplies are important for children with artistic abilities. Parents should allow and encourage free expression, exploration, discovery, learning, skills development, and new insights.

Things to avoid in order not to interfere with developing the child's gifts

In general, toddlers are prone to tantrums due to frustration. Gifted toddlers are even more likely to demonstrate this characteristic when their cognitive development outpaces their physical development and they can conceive of actions but cannot perform them. Parents should not punish such tantrums as they allow emotional venting and reduce tension. Researchers have found that parents who are overly directive and controlling tend to influence children to become less exploratory and curious, less independent and self-directed, less internally motivated, and less creative. Total permissiveness is not ideal, since children need appropriate limits, boundaries, structure, and guidance. Detached or uninvolved parents are not helpful. Parents should avoid punishing or disapproving of gifted children's actions as abnormal just for being unusual or unfamiliar. Parents should not avoid activities with their gifted children from insecurity regarding their own preparation or competence. Activities confer important bonding experiences as well as children's learning and positive reinforcement.

When a child exhibits giftedness in certain areas, the teacher should not prohibit or curtail the child's interest in preferred subjects and activities. If a gifted child prefers some subjects to the exclusion of other, required curriculum, the teacher can arrange behavioral contracts or contingencies; e.g., completing an assignment in a nonpreferred area can be rewarded with more time exploring a preferred interest. Teachers should not punish or disapprove extensive interest in certain subjects, a characteristic of gifted students. Teachers should not force gifted students to follow traditional procedures for learning and performing if they learn best with different procedures. As a student, Albert Einstein reputedly was failed in math by a teacher for not following the prescribed procedures, even though he got the right answers. Fortunately, he overcame this deterrent through his intellect, curiosity, and persistence. Teachers should not ignore gifted students who grow bored or who clamor for more material.

Clarifying effective practices

The National Research Center on Gifted and Talented (NRC/GT) is seeking to find out "what works in gifted education" through a five-year plan beginning with the 2008-2009 school year. Their plan involves integrating the examination of systems of identification, reading and math curricula based on theoretical models, and assessments of giftedness. Researchers are concentrating on three areas: (1) developing a solid system of identification that will build upon prior research; (2) with students identified via both traditional criteria and expanded criteria, analyzing the effects of certain units of reading and math curricula; and (3) measuring student outcomes using standardized achievement tests, extended standards-based assessments, or structured performance assessments. Researchers aim to create a system of identification for students across socioeconomic and cultural groups. Such groups will feature "talent pools" of elementary-school students, identified using standardized tests and teacher ratings, participating in randomly assigned reading and math curricula based on models.

Theoretical models of gifted instruction and in quantitative and qualitative research

By studying theories of gifted education, researchers study theoretical models to address areas that include: intelligence, identification, evaluation, alternative assessment, curriculum, programming, and professional development. Some common research questions among studies include these: Researchers want to know whether students from under-represented groups such as students with identified disabilities and abilities, students from economically disadvantaged populations, and Blacks and Latinos, will be identified in greater numbers by expanded criteria than by traditional criteria for identification. Researchers want to discover whether students identified as gifted by both traditional and non-traditional methods perform better on standardized achievement tests, extended standard-based assessments, and/or structured performance assessments when given the model-based curricula, than such students given their schools' general education curricula. Additionally, researchers want to know if students identified using traditional criteria outperform students identified by expanded criteria on standardized and performance-based measures.

Low-income black parents whose gifted children have achieved well in school

Various researchers have found that in low-income black families, the parents' amount of education did not influence their gifted children's achievement; rather, parents' attitudes and behaviors exerted the greatest influence on children's achievement. The parents of high-achieving students in this population assertively involved themselves in their children's education and kept track of the children's progress. These parents perceived themselves as competent in their coping skills and had optimistic attitudes. They established realistically high expectations for their gifted children. They supported the ideology of achievement, and their orientations toward achievement were positive. They established specific, clear, achievement-oriented norms for their children. They also created explicit and clear boundaries regarding roles. They purposefully practiced behaviors and provided experiences to promote their children's achievement. These parents' relationships with their gifted children were openly communicative, supportive, nurturing, trusting, respectful, and positive.

Low-income black parents whose gifted children were underachievers

Educational researchers have found that while low-income black gifted students who achieved well in school had parents with positive, optimistic attitudes and high expectations for their children's success, those students who underachieved academically had parents who did not feel as optimistic, expressing attitudes of helplessness and hopelessness. Parents of underachieving students in this population were less assertive about involvement in their children's educations than the parents of high-achieving students in this population. As a result, they were not as engaged in their children's schooling. Parents of these underachieving gifted black students were more likely to have unrealistic and/or unclear or ill-defined expectations for their children. These low-income black parents of gifted students who underachieved in school also were found to have less self-confidence in their parenting skills than parents of higher-achieving students in this population.

Education law

One function of government is education, which is administered through the public school system by the Federal Department of Education. The states, however, have primary responsibility for the maintenance and operation of public schools. The Federal Government does maintain a heavy interest, however, in education. The National Institute of Education was created to improve education in the United States.

Each state is required by its state constitution to provide a school system whereby children may receive an education, and state legislatures exercise power over schools in any manner consistent with the state's constitution. Many state legislatures delegate power over the school system to a state board of education.

Javits Act

The Javits Act, passed in 1988, after Public Law 94-142, aka the Education for All Handicapped Children Act (EHA) passed in 1975, renamed the Individuals with Disabilities Act (IDEA) in 1997, most recently reauthorized in 2004, with final regulations released in 2006. IDEA provides for all children to be educated, but it does not specify services for the gifted as for the disabled. The Javits Act, initiated by then-Senator Jacob Javits of New York, funds educational programs for gifted children from low-income families. It states, "The term gifted and talented student means children and youths who give evidence of higher performance capability in such areas as intellectual, creative, artistic, or leadership capacity, or in specific academic fields, and who require services or activities not ordinarily provided by the schools in order to develop such capabilities fully." This legislation meets the need for special services to gifted students in order to fulfill their special abilities.

Legal issues concerning gifted students

Federal laws protect the legal rights of students with disabilities but not the legal rights of gifted students without disabilities. Even the Jacob K. Javits Gifted and Talented Student Act (1994), which funds research and projects related to giftedness, does not protect gifted students' legal rights. Each U.S. state has jurisdiction over its educational procedures. However, discrimination based on giftedness is equally as unlawful as discrimination based on race, color, national origin, gender, or disability. Despite the lack of specific federal mandates for gifted education, the U.S. State Department of Education's Office of Civil Rights protects the educational rights of gifted students participating in government-funded programs and activities. From 1985-1995, this office has ruled in 86 cases involving gifted students regarding discrimination, identification, and program admissions. The American Civil Liberties Union has also filed discrimination suits; for example, against a school district for offering fewer Advanced Placement programs in schools with African-American and Hispanic populations with lower socioeconomic status.

Procedural safeguards for American state Departments of Education

Each state Department of Education writes its own procedural safeguards. Specifically, many states require that if parents obtain independent evaluations of their gifted children at their own private expense, the state's school districts must consider those evaluation findings in any educational decisions they make for those students. In addition, states commonly require that if an administrative law judge requests an independent evaluation as part of a hearing, the expense becomes a public responsibility. Usually the district must finance the evaluation. Another standard of state procedural safeguards, adopted from Federal disability laws, is the right of gifted students and their parents to a due process hearing regarding the student's identification, evaluation, or educational placement. States also commonly stipulate that students remain in their current placements while an administrative or judicial proceeding is pending.

Erikson's stages of social-emotional development

1. Learning Basic Trust vs. Basic Mistrust: The period of infancy in the first years of life where children who are loved and cared for develop trust and security. Children who are not become mistrustful and insecure.
2. Learning Autonomy vs. Shame: This occurs during early childhood, where the well-loved child welcomes his new sense of control, manifesting itself in tantrums, possessiveness, and the "no" and "mine" stage.
3. Learning Initiative vs. Guilt: A healthy child, usually up to school age, will develop his imagination, cooperate with others, and be both a leader and follower. A child who feels guilt will be fearful, not quite fit in socially, be dependent on adults, and have an underdeveloped imagination.
4. Industry vs. Inferiority: Entering school and up to junior high, the child will learn formal skills of life, initiate rules into free play, and desire self-discipline.
5. Learning Identity vs. Identity Diffusion: From adolescence to late teens, the child answers the question as to who he is, after

possibly going through rebellions and self-doubt. He may experiment with different roles, but anticipate achievement instead of feeling paralyzed by this process.

6. Learning Intimacy vs. Isolation: A successful young adult pursues true intimacy, whether it is in the form of long-lasting and enduring friendships or a partner for marriage.

7. Learning Generativity vs. Self-Absorption: Once adulthood is reached, whether in marriage or parenthood, the sense of working cooperatively and productively becomes of the utmost importance, rather than focusing only on independent goals.

8. Integrity vs. Despair: Once all other seven steps have been resolved, the mature adult reaches adjustment integrity. He can experiment after working hard and has developed a self-concept of which makes him happy and is proud of what he has created.

Piaget's developmental stages for children

1. Sensorimotor (birth to 2 years of age): Children build their set of concepts through physical interaction with their environment. They do not have the sense of object permanence that whereas to them it appears that the toy train ceases to exist when it is out of their sight, the toy train still exists.

2. Preoperational stage (ages 2-7): They still operate better in concrete situations. Although they may recognize abstract concepts, they are still unable to fully grasp them and their existence.

3. Concrete operations (ages 7-11): With more physical experiences, they can start to conceptualize, and may be able to solve abstract problems, such as using numbers in math instead of adding and subtracting physical objects.

4. Formal Operations (begins at 11-15): At this stage, children's cognitive structures are like those of an adult and include conceptual reasoning.

Processes of Identifying and Assessing Gifted and Talented Students

Assessment rubrics

Gifted and talented students tend to enjoy activities that they find stimulating and challenging. One way in which teachers can enhance their education is by offering students online educational games they can play wherein they apply the concepts they have learned in a lesson or unit. Online gaming has become so popular that it is a good choice for gifted students to extend and apply their knowledge and skills while having fun. For example, the About.com website has action games that address the content of various school subject areas. The Education World website's Online Game Archives has such games for students as Wacky Wordplay and Math Bingo. For teachers to evaluate student progress toward learning objectives they have developed for a unit, and evaluate the objectives themselves, they can find free assessment rubrics at websites like RubiStar. Teachers can customize RubiStar's rubric templates, including for assessment of virtual learning lessons/units.

Assessment rubrics are authentic assessment tools that are used to measure the work of students. It aims to evaluate a student's performance based on a set of criteria related to the task, rather than giving a single score for the work. Students usually receive the rubric before they attempt the task so that they know what is expected and for them to think about how the criteria will play out in their work. They can be analytic or holistic and are tailored to individual assessment tasks, allowing teachers to design the rubric for individual classes

and the needs of the students. Rubrics are also a formative type of assessment because it is an ongoing part of the teaching and learning process since it is revealed to the students before the assessment is even commenced.

Assessment strategies

An assessment is an illustrative task or opportunity to perform that targets the educational objectives for an assignment and allows students to demonstrate what they have learned and the progress of their learning. There are many strategies that can be used as strategies to assess student learning. Graphic organizers can allow the presentation of a variety of information or show how the information was obtained and learned. Interviewing others can provide a real life experience to a topic studied in class and put a face to the story and experience. Doing an observation can help students see how the topic appears in real life. If students complete self or peer evaluations, these can be useful because sometimes feedback from a peer group is more valuable than that of a teacher. Finally, portfolios can contain a little bit of everything and can track how the students have progressed through the assessment.

Performance-based assessment

Performance-based assessments are concerned with problem solving and understanding. The goal of this type of assessment is that students should be able to show their understanding of a topic studied that falls in line with certain curriculum goals. These types of assessment can provide a measure of achievement as well as track a teacher's progress with an individual student. They could take the form of essays, oral presentations, open-ended problems, role-playing or hands-on tasks. It could also take the form of a portfolio that students put together throughout the study of a certain topic that shows how their learning has taken place over a period of study. Self-evaluation also has a place in performance-based assessment as the students often have to be critical of themselves and the process it took them to get to the finished result.

Quantitative measurement

A quantitative measurement uses results from an instrument based on a standardized system that limits the collection of data to a preset amount of possible responses. This is more commonly known as a standardized test, such as the ACT or SAT to get into college, or any test with multiple choice responses. This type of measurement is more concerned with the details of performance and can be used as both a pre-and post-subject assessment of performance after knowledge on a certain topic has been studied. When these tests are given in the classroom, they can be more effective if a more experienced teacher has created the test in order to ensure that concepts are being tested, not just facts and ideas.

Quantitative measurement vs. performance-based assessment

Both types of assessment have their place in the classroom, as long as they are used accurately. It would not be useful, for example, to have a multiple-choice test after having students read a book in order to show their interpretation of a book. It would, however, be appropriate to have a standardized test regarding vocabulary or the background to a novel, to then be taken after the text to see how much the students have learned. Performance-based assessment tends to be more individually driven by each student and by that fact alone it tends to be a more exciting form of assessment. However, it requires a lot of thought on the teacher's

part in order to make sure that all the choices are relevant to the topic and can be graded on some sort of scale.

Alternative means of assessment

By having a variety of products that the students can produce, they will be more likely to choose something that catches their interest, therefore having some intrinsic motivation to do well at the task. The product can be varied in complexity depending upon what ability level upon which each student is working. Students who are working below grade level may have the performance expectations reduced, whereas students who are working above grade level may be asked to demonstrate higher and more complex learning processes in their adaptation of the product. By giving the students the choice of what they are working on, a natural differentiation occurs because each student will automatically adjust the task to his ability level.

Assessment of students with dual exceptionalities

Identification of giftedness in students who are disabled is problematic. The customary identification methods (i.e., standardized tests and observational checklists) are inadequate without major modification. Standard lists of characteristics of gifted students may be inadequate for unmasking hidden potential in children who have disabilities. Children whose hearing is impaired, for example, cannot respond to oral directions, and they may also lack the vocabulary which reflects the complexity of their thoughts. Children whose speech or language is impaired cannot respond to tests requiring verbal responses. Children whose vision is impaired may be unable to respond to certain performance measures, and although their vocabulary may be quite advanced, they may not understand the full meaning of the words they use (e.g., color words). Children with learning disabilities may use high-level vocabulary in speaking but be unable to express themselves in writing, or vice versa. In addition, limited life experiences due to impaired mobility may artificially lower scores. Because the population of gifted/disabled students is difficult to locate, they are seldom included in standardized test norming groups, adding to the problems of comparison. In addition, gifted children with disabilities often use their intelligence to try to circumvent the disability. This may cause both exceptionalities to appear less extreme; using one to mask the other normalizes both.

Standard error of measurement

Standard error of measurement is the estimate of the 'error' associated with the test-taker's obtained score when compared with their hypothetical 'true' score. The SEM, which varies from test to test, should be given in the test manual. The band of scores in which we can be fairly certain the 'true' score lies can be calculated from this figure.

Raw score and scaled score

Raw score is an original datum that has not been transformed. A standard score is a dimensionless quantity derived from the raw score.

Scaled score is a standardized score, that is, it is based upon the normal distribution and standard deviation units.

Mastery level

Mastery levels are the cutoff score on a criterion-referenced or mastery test; people who score at or above the cutoff score are considered to have mastered the material; mastery may be an arbitrary judgment.

Syncretism

Syncretism is the conscious adopting of the cultural elements of a dominant group by a subordinate group. One classic example of this kind of syncretism is the economic transformation of Japan after World War Two. The Japanese, with help from the Western powers, rapidly developed an industrial base and market economy modeled after that of the United States. Syncretism has often been used to describe the interplay of religions within a society; for example, it is invoked hopefully by those who would like to see reconciliation between the Protestant and Catholic churches. Sociologists note that there is a danger in syncretism of losing elements of culture that are unique to the subordinate culture, and thus discouraging debate and innovation.

Grade equivalent score

What the grade equivalent score actually measures is how typical students at the grade level specified would perform on the test that has been given. In other words, a 4th grader's grade equivalent of 10.4 does not indicate that the 4th grade is capable of doing 10th grade work. Rather, it indicates that the 4th grade student has performed as well as a typical 10th grade student would have performed on the 4th grade test. If the student is performing on grade level, that is a 4th grade student taking the test in the 10th month of 4th grade receives a score of 4.10, then it simply indicates that he/she is performing right at the average for other 4th graders in the norming sample, which is the 50th percentile and 50th NCE. Grade equivalents do not lend themselves to measuring aggregate performance of all students in a school or school district, nor do they average well and are hard to understand when dealing with groups. Accordingly, the score used more often is the Normal Curve Equivalent, or NCE.

Testing modifications

Directions

Key words could be underlined by the teacher, or the teacher could read the directions aloud and ask if there are any questions before beginning.

Adapted Expectations

The grading scale could be altered to account for students with lower cognitive functioning that may know some of the concepts, but not all of them.

Time constraints

Extended test time with supervision could be determined to be appropriate depending on the student and his IEP.

Essay questions

Completing an outline could be an option, or having the student verbalize answers onto a tape recorder, or having someone else transcribe his answers.

Additional tools

For some tests, formulas, sample problems, dictionaries or computers may be used in order to facilitate the test-taking process.

Assessment station

An assessment station is a designated area, inside or outside of the classroom, used for the specific purpose of evaluating students' progress performing a task. Individuals or groups can be assigned to complete a task, use a piece of lab equipment or work with some technological device. The purpose is to assess the knowledge acquired, processes used, skills displayed and general attitude about the task and, if working in a group, how each student interacts with the other members of the team. The assessment station should function the same way every time it is used. This builds consistency and reduces the time needed for explanations and demonstrations

before and during future assessments. Instructions should be clear, concise and specific and explain exactly how the area should be left for the next student. Activities performed in the assessment station should be simple, straightforward and relate to the material being studied.

Because the assessment station is an interactive tool, the area needs to be equipped with the appropriate equipment necessary to complete the task. If the activity is an experiment, the area needs to be ventilated and appropriate safety precautions taken, e.g., having water available and a fire extinguisher at hand. The students need to understand how to operate the instruments in a safe manner and therefore instructions should be provided both in writing and verbally. Questions should be asked and answered before any activity is started. If it is a group activity, each student needs to contribute to the assigned task. The work submitted by each student is evaluated using a rating/grading scale or a checklist. For example if the task required the use of a microscope, the checklist should have points related to its use. If it was a group project, cooperation, helpfulness and leadership skills should be noted.

Individual assessments

Individual assessments focus on the progress each student made during a defined period of time (e.g., every six weeks, at the end of the semester) rather than in a team collaboration. A variety of activities such as written assignments, oral presentations and class participation should be incorporated into the assessment in order to obtain a broader, more realistic view of the student's understanding of the material. The assessment process should be fully explained so that the student knows that which is expected. He is evaluated using one or all of the following standards:

- self-referenced —based on his previous level of progress
- criterion-referenced — a defined, school or district-wide standard
- norm-referenced — based on the progress of groups of students the same age or grade level

Using a combination of standards instead of relying on one method presents a clearer, more accurate picture of the student's growth.

Individual assessments are easily understood by students and parents and mesh with most school districts' systems. Because each student is evaluated based on criteria established by state performance and/or content standards, it is easy to measure the success of department curricula. Self-referenced standards provide feedback about the student's strengths and weaknesses. They can help motivate the student to work harder and take more responsibility for his learning. Students sometimes set personal goals and expectations. Individual assessments help them measure their success. These evaluations provide the teacher insight into any special help the student might need. Individual assessment can create and encourage a very competitive environment in which some students are unable to compete effectively. It makes it difficult to evaluate students' ability to work with a team and judge their interaction with others both of which are important to the educational experience. They can also be also very time-consuming for the teacher to complete fairly and accurately.

Group assessments

Group assessments focus on how students cooperate and collaborate in completing a project assigned to the group rather than to a single student. The same activities used in individual assessments are used—namely, written assignments, oral presentations and group participation—but they are used to evaluate social and interactive skills as well as the work produced. The students' willingness to accept being evaluated for a group project is based on if and how long they have been exposed to this type of cooperative collaboration and if they feel the grading system is applied fairly. If this project is the first time students in a competitive environment are expected to work together, there may be some misunderstandings and objections about what is expected, how it works and how each student will be evaluated. It is critical the teacher explains the evaluation process clearly, answers questions, addresses reservations and closely monitors individual contributions as well as the progress of the project.

There are three ways to evaluate a group project: group grade only, individual grade only, or a combination of both. The reason for group projects is to teach cooperation in a team environment and therefore giving everyone the same grade can foster some degree of esprit de corps. It also frees the teacher from having to decide who was responsible for what part of the project. A group grade, however, can cause resentment, especially if students are not used to working in a group and are used to earning grades based on a competitive scale. Students understand individual grades but in a group project environment the competitive scale diminishes the spirit of cooperation because everyone is working for himself rather than for the good of the team. Giving a group grade and an individual grade addresses both issues. Basing eighty percent of the grade on cooperation and collaboration and twenty percent on individual production recognizes the importance of working for the group and the necessity of individual contributions.

Performance contracts

Performance contracts can be a great learning experience for students by teaching them how to plan and prioritize and encouraging them to avoid procrastination. However, some students may have trouble understanding the concept so it may be necessary to review the planning, organizing and writing steps several times before they are able to grasp the idea. Using contracts can also help a struggling student in other areas of his life. These agreements can be developed to address attendance requirements and expected behavior standards or to plan weekly or monthly homework schedules. If a teacher has never used performance contracts, he needs to understand that setting up the system and helping the students write their agreements is very time consuming, especially in the beginning. It can help, as a class project, to create a performance contract based on a completed project. This strategy sometimes reduces the learning curve for all the students.

A performance contract is a written agreement between an individual student or a group of students and a teacher about a specific activity. The assignment can be a research paper, an oral presentation with props or some other project. The contract clearly states the goal, explains the activity, establishes a timeline and describes who will do what and how it will be done. Sometimes the agreement also details the criteria to be used to evaluate the finished product. This tool helps students learn to plan a project by breaking it into manageable parts and shows them how to utilize their time more efficiently. Not only can the completed project be graded, but the performance contract itself can be evaluated. The teacher should assess the student's participation in setting up the contract, his willingness to compromise when necessary and his general attitude about the concept and the process.

In order for a performance contract to be a learning experience, the guidelines for writing one should be very general. The teacher can either give the student a written list of suggestions or, preferably, discuss them one-on-one. Some questions that might be used:
- What work items are you planning to include?
- Where you will find the necessary data? Personal reference books? The Internet? The library? Do you have additional sources?
- How long will it take to outline a plan, research the topic, and finish the project?
- What criteria should be used to evaluate the finished product?

Questions that might be used to evaluate the completed contract:
- Is the contract realistic relative to required completion date?
- Are the contract questions appropriate to the project objectives?
- Were reliable and appropriate sources chosen?
- How comprehensive is the plan?
- Does the student understand his capabilities and recognize his limitations?

Naglieri Nonverbal Ability Test®, 2nd edition (NNAT®-2)

According to the test's author, the NNAT®-2 is "culturally neutral," thereby making it suitable for testing culturally diverse student populations. It is nonverbal, making it a good choice for ESL/ELL and nonverbal students. It can be used with ages 5 through 17 years and grades K through 12. It has seven levels corresponding to grades K; 1; 2; 3-4; 5-6; 7-9; and 10-12. It takes 30 minutes and is easy to administer. Students do not need good reading skills, math skills, well-developed vocabularies, or factual knowledge to respond to the test items. For identifying gifted/talented students whose socioeconomic backgrounds have limited their development of verbal skills and acquisition of information, this test is a useful instrument. Among tests of ability, the NNAT®-2 has the most recent norms, from 2008. Its administration and instructions are facilitated by pictures. Its graduated difficulty range allows identification of advanced as well as gifted and talented students.

The NNAT®-2 offers both pencil-and-paper and online administration options. The online version saves teachers and administrators a great deal of time compared with the time required for the pencil-and-paper version. It also saves money, as schools do not have to pay for printed paper tests. Furthermore, this test saves time, space, money, and human energy by relieving schools of the need for storing, distributing, organizing, and shipping test booklets. It has minimal system requirements, enabling more users and computers to access it. The test's publisher, Pearson, uses a secure browser, protecting the safety of student information. Paperless, this test offers a more environmentally friendly option than does the traditional paper-and-pencil test. The online version yields instant results, allowing teachers to spend more time with students requiring additional, more focused instruction. Online reporting allows teachers to tailor data disaggregation and filtering to their district's needs. The online format is appealing and motivating to students, promoting test completion for fuller measurement. One item per screen helps students focus.

Full-Scale IQ (FSIQ) score on the Wechsler Intelligence Scales for Children, 4th edition (WISC-IV, 2003)

Researchers at the Gifted Development Center observe that since the WISC-IV includes more emphasis on processing skills than earlier versions, this confounds the identification of giftedness because gifted students tend to score higher on abstract thinking measures but lower on processing measures. This characteristic reflects the asynchronous development typical of gifted children. Averaging these measures lowers the FSIQ score. The researchers find abstract thought a better index of intelligence than processing speed or working memory. They also point out that many educators mistakenly assume gifted students are naturally quicker processors. Some are, but many others are perfectionists and/or reflective thinkers, which slows down processing time. Also, many gifted students perform well on meaningful tasks, but not on tests of short-term memory containing material with no meaning for them. Flanagan and Kaufman (2004) recommend not reporting the FSIQ score if the difference between the highest and lowest Composite scores is 23 points or more.

According to a number of educational researchers who have analyzed its content and results, the WISC-IV is a useful diagnostic tool for giftedness. They note that although it seldom gives scores above the 140s and has a score ceiling of 160, it also indicates ability beyond these limits. WISC-IV's ten required subtests include: Similarities, Vocabulary, Comprehension, Matrix Reasoning, Picture Concepts, Block Design, Letter-Number Sequencing, Symbol Search, Digit Span, and Coding. Optional supplementary subtests include: Arithmetic, Word Reasoning, Picture Completion, and Cancellation. The WISC-IV gives four Composite Scores from

- 26 -

subscale groups: Verbal Comprehension, Perceptual Reasoning, Working Memory, and Processing Speed. Expert analyses find Verbal Comprehension (a composite of Similarities, Vocabulary, and Comprehension subscales) and Perceptual Reasoning (a composite of Matrix Reasoning, Picture Concepts, and Block Design subscales) very good indications of giftedness, as they assess abstract and visual thinking. Working Memory and Processing Speed are the subscales least correlated with giftedness.

At the Gifted Development Center, Silverman, Gilman, and Falk (2004) found that gifted students' WISC-IV Composite Scores in Verbal Comprehension and Perceptual Reasoning were typically high enough to qualify them for gifted educational services, but their scores on Working Memory and Processing Speed subscales were typically below qualifying levels. Additionally, since the Full-Scale IQ (FSIQ) score average incorporates these lower scores, they drag the average down, and also are individually not good indicators of giftedness. Consequently, the FSIQ identifies neither gifted strengths nor relative weaknesses. The DWI-1 computes a score combining the Verbal Comprehension and Perceptual Reasoning Composites using only six WISC-IV subscales, which these researchers find an excellent option for schools to identify gifted students. Flanagan and Kaufman's GAI averages the same two Composite scores; Harcourt Assessments (PsychCorp) trainers support this. Another solution involves basing identification on assessments of reasoning, delivering gifted services/accommodations, and adding accommodations for relative weaknesses.

The Arithmetic subscale of the WISC-IV is found the strongest indicator of general intelligence (g); (Keith et al, 2004) and the strongest index of giftedness (Silverman, Gilman, and Falk, 2004).

Vocabulary, Information, and Similarities, in that order, were identified by Keith et al as the next best indices of g. "Fair" measures of g were the Matrix Reasoning, Block Design, Word Reasoning, Comprehension, Letter-Number Sequencing, Picture Completion, Picture Concepts, Symbol Search, and Digit Span subscales, in that order. They found the Coding subscale "poor," and the Cancellation subscale the "poorest" measure of g. While Keith et al ranked Letter-Number Sequencing higher than Digit Span in their factor loading on g, Silverman and colleagues note that student responses to Digit Span are more predictable and interpretable, whereas Letter-Number Sequencing can seriously confuse and slow down some gifted students. They sometimes substitute Arithmetic for Letter-Number Sequencing with non-math-phobic students.

Researchers at the Gifted Development Center recommend, often subscales required by the WISC-IV, using only the following six to identify giftedness: Vocabulary, Similarities, Comprehension, Matrix Reasoning, Picture Concepts, and Block Design. The first three subscales comprise the Verbal Comprehension Index; the last three subscales comprise the Perceptual Reasoning Index. The researchers find these two indices most relevant to measuring giftedness. The General Ability Index (GAI) is recommended by Flanagan and Kaufman (2004) as an additional measure, computed from the six subscales/two indices named. Dumont and Willis provided the Dumont-Willis Indices (DWI); the DWI-1 is similar to the GAI, computed from the Verbal Comprehension and Perceptual Reasoning indices. The DWI-2 averages Working Memory and Processing Speed. They advise only computing both DWI-1 and DWI-2 for gifted students if scores are similar. Advantages include greater efficiency, time- and cost-effectiveness, and accuracy without Working Memory and Processing Speed scores, which confound results for gifted students

Verbal comprehension and perceptual reasoning with the areas of working memory and processing speed

Researchers compared Wechsler Intelligence Scale for Children (WISC-IV) scores of a gifted student group with scores of a control group from the WISC-IV's normative sample. The normative sample had little IQ variation—only 4 points between highest and lowest subscale scores. Working Memory and Processing Speed scores were not lower enough than Verbal Comprehension and Perceptual Reasoning scores to lower their Full-Scale IQ (FSIQ) averages. In contrast, the gifted sample averaged 27.4 points difference between highest and lowest subscale scores; the greatest variation was 69 points—over four standard deviations. Almost 60% of gifted students had 23-point differences between Verbal Comprehension and Processing Speed Composites. Gifted students scored 25 points higher than the norm group in Verbal Comprehension, but differed by below 2 points in Processing Speed. This trend implies gifted students are superior in verbal abstract reasoning but not processing; as a result, the WISC-IV's FSIQ should not be used for gifted identification.

Gifted Rating Scales (GRS) (Pfeiffer and Jarosowich, 2003)

The GRS are norm-referenced, based on a multidimensional model of giftedness, and informed by current giftedness theories as well as federal and state definitions and guidelines. The GRS-P form, for ages 4 years to 6 years, 11 months, includes domains of intellect, academic readiness, motivation, creativity, and artistic talent. The GRS-S form, for ages 6:0 through 13:11 and

grades 1-8, includes the same five domains as the GRS-P, except for an academic domain rather than academic readiness and the additional sixth domain of leadership. Administration takes 5-10 minutes. Relative strengths and specific gifted areas can be identified. Statistical validity studies positively correlate the GRS with the Wechsler Preschool and Primary Scales of Intelligence (WPPSI-III), Wechsler Intelligence Scales for Children (WISC-IV), and Wechsler Individual Achievement Test (WIAT-II). These standardized scales are designed to help qualify students for placement in gifted/talented programs. Domain-specific identification guidelines are included. Teacher form completion is easy and quick.

Wechsler Preschool and Primary Scales of Intelligence (WPPSI-III)

The WPPSI-III is for ages 2.6 to 7.3 years. It includes 14 subscales: Block Design, Information, Matrix Reasoning, Vocabulary, Picture Concepts, Symbol Search, Word Reasoning, Coding, Comprehension, Picture Completion, Similarities, Receptive Vocabulary, Object Assembly, and Picture Naming. By various combinations of subtests, measures can be computed for verbal IQ, performance (fluid) IQ, processing speed quotient, general language composite, and full-scale IQ. Verbal IQ, performance IQ, and full-scale IQ are computed from core subtests. The WPPSI-III features short activities to accommodate attention spans of the youngest children in the age range. Activities are colorful and game-like, appealing to and interesting young children. Varied samples, second chances, and layered scoring enabling partial credit help children do their best. With children aged 6.0-7.3, the WISC-IV, for ages 6:0-16:11, is recommended for identifying giftedness, the WPPSI-III for general academic reasons. Because they are similar, these should not be administered successively to avoid practice effects.

Multi-Dimensional Screening Device (MDSD)

The MDSD (Kranz, 1978) is based on the idea that intelligence is multidimensional in nature, not reflected by any one measurement. The author designed this instrument to facilitate better initial identification of giftedness among "the less accepted school population." A staff development program for teachers required to participate in the screening process is part of this instrument. In fact, the first step in its implementation is staff development. Other steps include rating students individually and forming a local screening committee to select individual students for screening. The MDSD's categories of giftedness are: visual arts ability; performing arts ability; demonstrated creative/productive thinking; discipline-specific academic ability; general intellectual ability of 1 in 100 or more; leadership characteristics, organization, and decision-making; psychomotor history and ability; history and use of spatial and abstract thought; wide difference between performance and general intellectual ability; and talent related to cultural heritage.

Wechsler Preschool and Primary Scales of Intelligence (WPPSI-III) as an assessment

The WPPSI-III is a standardized instrument with proven validity and reliability. However, it does have some disadvantages. In testing the youngest children, the WPPSI-III's subscales reflect an expectation for IQ scores to jump significantly every 2-3 months. To qualify children for gifted services, experts advise scheduling testing optimally for ruling in/out such qualification. They also warn that a retest can take up to two years, so if a child has taken the WPPSI-III and needs re-evaluation sooner, they should use a different test. Another consideration about the WPPSI related to the youngest children is that IQ results are not as stable at earlier ages. Therefore, administering the WPPSI-III near the end of the kindergarten year is recommended to allow greater maturation and pre-academic/academic skills development. An exception is when earlier testing is indicated, e.g. a child displays signs of extreme giftedness at a very young age.

Identification, assessment, and eligibility for services

While federal law provides that students with designated disabilities are guaranteed a free appropriate public education (FAPE), it does not address gifted students. Thus each individual determines the procedural safeguards for gifted students' identification, assessment, and eligibility for services, just as each state also determines its definition of giftedness and gifted programs. Some examples of procedural safeguards include: requiring school districts to give parents prior written notice before identifying, evaluating, placing, changing, or providing a FAPE to their child; obtaining written parental informed consent before initially evaluating their child to determine eligibility and before initially providing services for gifted children; parents' right to examine their child's school records and participate in educational planning meetings for their child; parents' right to due process hearings to resolve disputes related to identification, evaluation, or placement of their child or provision of a FAPE; and many others.

Test ceiling

A test ceiling means a test's upper limit, i.e. the highest score it is capable of yielding. Most intelligence and achievement tests used in schools cannot accurately measure gifted student levels if they exceed the limits the test can measure. For example, many IQ and achievement tests direct administrators to stop when the student gets three consecutive items wrong.   The disadvantage: a student can get two wrong, one right, one wrong, etc., never meeting the stopping criterion of three wrong consecutively. The student does miss a number of items, yet never hits the test's ceiling. An additional disadvantage: the student never reaches the point when items become too difficult to answer, which represents the true ceiling. Therefore, that student's score may be accurate, a bit too low, or much too low, but this is impossible to determine.   Only certain is that the student's score is his/her lowest possible score.

Facilitating Growth and Learning in Gifted and Talented Students

Developing an IEP

In part because federal law addresses special education needs for disabled students but not for gifted students, in part because of emphases on inclusive education, and for other reasons, most public schools do not have many (or any) classrooms with all gifted students. Many schools have pull-out gifted programs, which comprise a very small part (about 5%) of the gifted students' school hours. Thus, the general classroom should be the focal area for modifications or accommodations included in a gifted IEP. In addition, if any school problems arise in gifted students, such problems are likely to arise in regular classrooms. Gifted students who learn more quickly and/or with less repetition can become bored and/or impatient with the class pace and come to dislike school. Although such problems may be minor in elementary school, they still should be addressed early to prevent the development of larger problems by high school. Simple general classroom changes in gifted IEPs can make tremendous differences.

Issues with gifted education and IEPs

Many parents of gifted children have commonly expressed several repeated experiences across public school districts. First, many parents report being told that their children must make up assignments in the general education classroom they missed due to the gifted pull-out program. Furthermore, some parents are told that since their child earns As in school, s/he needs no special attention or supplementary educational services. Parents often express concern that their child is growing comfortable with levels of schoolwork too low for his/her ability, that school is not offering challenges to their child, and/or that their child is developing bad study habits. Many parents are surprised and disappointed that their school district seems averse or avoidant to acknowledge and address their child's giftedness, since parents often expect for school districts to welcome superior learners. Parents often express perplexity or resentment at not knowing about available educational programming for their gifted children.

Two main concepts regarding gifted education (as expressed by McIntyre and Mery, 2004) are: (1) educationally, "gifted" does not mean that a student necessarily demonstrates superior academic performance in the regular, general education classroom. Rather, it means that the student has an educational need. The gifted child learns differently enough from others that regular classroom, grade-level teaching methods and practices are insufficient. (2) Once this educational need is identified, the school must plan for the student's individual education to meet his or her specific needs. This planning is reflected in the development of an IEP. In addition to the need to individualize the student's educational planning, the authors emphasize that gifted "pull-out" programs alone are insufficient, as students still spend around 95% of their time in regular classes. Pull-outs should be used together with modifications to the regular program. Also, accommodations/services must not be limited to group programs, precluding individualization.

Recurring issues that many parents of gifted students in public school districts have reported include the following: when invited to IEP meetings, many parents report they were not informed of their status as equal partners in IEP planning, not informed that IEP meetings are working meetings, or not informed that parents should bring their own ideas to meetings. Many parents report they were not informed that accommodations to general classrooms could be written in gifted IEPs. If parents find their school has not assessed a student's present level of educational performance, many express that they were not informed how to request testing or that assessment results could be used to develop their child's gifted IEP. Parents often state they are told that acceleration in grade or subject violates the school district's policy, and that their gifted program is an "enrichment only" program. They also say districts often indicate their pull-out program as their entire gifted program.

IEP planning meeting

A gifted IEP planning meeting should be student-centered and should be used for developing the IEP, not simply for reviewing a previously written IEP with no input from the meeting. Because school IEP team members will have prepared for the meeting, parents may misinterpret this preparation as the school presenting a predetermined plan. However, all members, including the parents and the student, should contribute to IEP development during the meeting. If a certain class or pull-out program is proposed, for example, but parents know it will not challenge their child (or already does not), they should indicate this. If parents find that the proposed IEP does not meet a certain educational need for their child, they should bring this up for the school to define and the team to find ways to meet it. Parents also can advocate for courses initially not offered by the school or not at their child's grade level.

Children's school records

Parents have the right to request and receive copies of all of their children's school records, including the results of any tests. These may not all be in one place. For example, the guidance counselor might maintain records of students' IEPs and educational programs, while IQ and other test results would be maintained by the school psychologist. Gifted advocates advise that parents of gifted students should obtain copies of current tests used to identify their child as gifted and of tests used to determine the student's achievement levels. Common misconceptions among all parents, including those with gifted children, is that the school IEP team already has created the IEP, that it cannot be altered, and that they are attending the meeting only to review and approve/disapprove its content. As such, parents must be informed of their roles as equal team members in contributing to, developing, and/or modifying their child's gifted IEP.

Present Levels of Educational Performance (PLEP)

Generally, objective assessments are needed to establish a student's PLEP. While subjective teacher observations, or checklists showing student strengths and weaknesses in the curriculum, are helpful for developing a gifted IEP, they should not be used to define PLEP, which requires objective testing instruments for accuracy. Ideally, such objective measurements are taken at least annually, or more often as needed. However, in the reality of public schools, this schedule is seldom followed with gifted students. Gifted IEP teams often wrongly use report cards, which measure learning of material taught in the past rather than in the present,, and do not indicate student ability—a student may get As in a class which is still three grade levels below his/her capacity, or a student may be so uninterested in this lower level as to get Cs or even Fs. Either way, the student would not be functioning at his/her present level of educational performance.

Main parts of a Gifted IEP

When developing a Gifted IEP (or any IEP in general), the first part should indicate the student's Present Levels of Educational Performance (PLEP). Because asynchronous development is characteristic of gifted students, they have relative strengths and weaknesses as other do students, and they also may be extremely gifted in specific areas. Therefore the PLEP must reflect school performance in all school subjects. This establishes a baseline wherefrom subsequent educational programming proceeds. The second IEP part should state the student's educational goals. Goals are more general and global; they do not include specific ways of achieving them. A third IEP part includes short-term learning objectives. These objectives do specify the time frames in which to achieve them and exactly what measures will demonstrate the learning. These are steps in achieving goals. A fourth part outlines specially designed instruction for the gifted student and explains teaching methods for attaining student short-term outcomes and long-term goals.

Goals vs. objectives

Goals are the long-term targets for a student's education, while objectives represent short-term targets, but this is not the only difference. Goals need not be specific or measurable, whereas objectives should be both specific and measurable. While goals are more general and global, they still must be specific to the individual student rather than assigned to that student based on his or her class or group. First, identifying the individual student's educational needs and the final outcomes desired are the ways of determining the student's educational goals. Short-term learning objectives then specify the smaller steps the student must achieve toward eventually meeting the associated goal. Objectives are also the IEP team's means of measuring student progress toward a goal. Objectives quantify criteria for attainment and state when these criteria are to be met. Goals and objectives should be congruent with one another: when read together, they should "make sense" to parents as well as to educators.

Above grade level

By itself, the phrase "above grade level" contributes no meaning to establishing a gifted student's Present Levels of Educational Performance (PLEP) or to developing that student's IEP. Some gifted advocates opine this phrase should not be included in gifted IEPs. If it does appear, both the student's current grade level in school and the grade level at which the student performs must be defined. In some U.S. states, State Departments of Education require these determinations by law. Objective, standardized achievement tests have established norms for each grade level, so these definitions can be determined through test scores and norms. The description "above grade level" without such specific grade-level information is analogous to going clothes shopping for a child with only the information that s/he is "taller than four feet." The child's actual height must be measured; so must the student's actual performance grade level be measured, as well.

What the gifted IEP is and is not for the teacher

In general, the gifted IEP is a guide for the teacher to help focus instruction on the student's educational needs and goals. It is not a rigid directive forcing the teacher to adhere to specific activities determined months before instruction. At the beginning of the school year, the student's gifted IEP should establish the student's main educational goals and a schedule within the school year for their attainment. Because goals are more general than short-term learning objectives, they allow time for teacher and student to collaborate in determining a school subject for a given goal that is compatible with the student's abilities and preferences. After arriving at a subject, the teacher and student can collaborate further in developing individual short-term learning objectives according to the schedule previously established. These objectives specify the smaller increments/steps toward achieving a goal, permitting the teacher to adjust to the student while also assuring progress.

Conducting the Gifted IEP (GIEP) meeting with parents

For a GIEP meeting, educators typically will prepare some provisional educational goals, courses, and activities they deem appropriate for the student. Furthermore, educators should avoid using technical jargon so parents can understand it. Parents should bring their ideas to the meeting. They can inform educators of their child's interests, likes and dislikes, and behavior, and bring suggestions for educational programs and/or materials they want for their child. They also should ask questions about anything they do not understand or if they need more information. When educators present parents at the meeting's end with a document to sign, often called a Notice of Recommended Assignment (NORA), parents should not assume they must sign it immediately. State laws allow a number of days for them to decide. Parents can request additional and/or amended wording. They can also write exceptions

to parts they do not accept, and then sign, or they can reject the entire GIEP.

Relationship of the general education teacher to the Gifted IEP (GIEP)

If a gifted student is in a general education classroom for any part of the school day, the general education teacher needs to be familiar with the content of the student's GIEP. None of the privacy laws protecting the privacy/confidentiality of student records applies to either general or gifted education teachers' access to the GIEP. Some school districts have their own privacy procedures, such as having general education teachers sign a log to read a GIEP, but teachers are still allowed to read the GIEP. They cannot align with the GIEP's goals, objectives, activities, and materials without knowing them. Familiarity with the GIEP facilitates general teachers' coordinating their instruction with gifted teachers/programs. If parents believe their child's teacher does not know about the GIEP, and/or that their child is identified as gifted, they should ask the teacher. Bringing their child's gifted written report and GIEP to parent-teacher conferences is advisable.

Addressing education in both gifted and general education programs

Gifted children do not have gifts only part of the time; they are the same individuals all the time. As a result, their educational needs also are constant. Such rationale also extends for addressing those needs throughout the school day/year. Each school district has the responsibility not only to place a gifted student in a gifted program, but also to make whatever accommodations and modifications in the regular education setting, curriculum, and instructional methods are necessary and specified in the gifted IEP (GIEP) to meet the student's individual educational needs. Parents should know that if district administrators tell them a gifted pull-out program is the "only" accommodation available, this constitutes a severe misrepresentation of the district's responsibilities and the student's and parents' rights. Parents should inform administrators they are aware of these responsibilities and rights and should hold administrators responsible for addressing and fulfilling these rights. Parents can advocate for their child at GIEP meetings and/or request due process hearings.

Specially Designed Instruction (SDI)

The Specially Designed Instruction (SDI) section of the GIEP is, in general, the section where classroom activities are designed to match the individual gifted student's needs. Any specific educational challenges or issues for that student, including any problems the student has in the general education classroom, should be addressed here. Any educational programming that the student and his/her parents think should become part of the school district's gifted program should also be included in the SDI section. Three considerations relative to general education teachers and GIEPs are: (1) gifted education and general education for gifted students are not separate entities: gifted students' needs must be met in BOTH district gifted programs AND general education classrooms; (2) general education teachers cannot refuse to implement GIEPs; parents have recourse (i.e. another GIEP meeting/due process) if teachers do refuse to implement; and (3) general education teachers have access to all parts of GIEPs.

GIEP meeting procedures and parent recourse if a teacher refuses to implement a GIEP

Advocates observe that engaging general education teachers in the GIEP process represents the best way of developing and implementing a GIEP. The general education teacher should attend the GIEP meeting. Since a teacher familiar with the student always should attend IEP meetings, the primary general education teacher also is likely to be on the IEP team and attend the meeting. If a school/district does not include the general education teacher, parents can request the chairperson of the GIEP team or local educational agency (LEA) to include her/him. All teachers must comply with the GIEP. If a teacher refuses to implement the whole GIEP or any part(s) of it, e.g. pre-testing, giving differentiated classwork and/or homework, etc., parents either should call for another Team meeting or pursue due process proceedings. Teachers can make written objections to a GIEP on record. However, team-proposed, parent-approved GIEPs always must be implemented.

Instructional accommodations that can be requested

The only constraints on accommodations one might request in school for a gifted student are that such accommodations be reasonably expected to provide the student with meaningful educational value using the school's curriculum. Any accommodations meeting these criteria can be written into a student's gifted IEP. A common response from school/district administrators for students, parents, and advocates to consider is that no one ever has asked for a certain accommodation before, or no others are requesting a particular change. This happens more frequently in schools using only pull-out gifted services and/or those schools not normally providing accommodations to general education classrooms. Administrative responses even can give students/parents/advocates the impression that their request is inconvenient and/or unnecessary.

However, rejecting a request simply because it sets a precedent is not valid. The only criteria for validity are the reasonable expectation of meaningful educational value and its educational appropriateness for the individual student.

Differentiated homework

Since gifted students most often are placed in general education classrooms and given supplementary gifted services, they could be assigned the same homework as the regular class, plus another set of homework from their gifted program. Thus, gifted students can end up feeling punished rather than rewarded by having to complete a double amount of homework. Differentiated homework can avoid this problem by substituting homework more appropriate to the student's gifts instead of the regular class homework rather than in addition to it. Differentiated homework also can eliminate excessive rote work/repetition beyond the gifted student's needs. For example, assigning math puzzles instead of memorization lets gifted students apply their knowledge. Assigning a gifted student an additional vocabulary list, with homework only on the extra list, and/or having a gifted student write two longer stories per week instead of five shorter stories are other examples.

Independent study agreements

In public schools, gifted students are not commonly enrolled in completely separate gifted programs/"tracks" where all classes differ from general education classes in order to accommodate the gifted students' learning needs. Such gifted students most often are placed in general education classrooms for part/all of the school day. They may have pull-out programs for gifted instruction, but such programs represent a minority of the student's school day/week. Due to asynchronous development, some gifted students are farther ahead of the regular curriculum in some subjects than in others. Also, some gifted students still may find the regular curriculum relevant, but they simply may finish their classwork sooner. Independent study agreements offer gifted students ways to occupy their free time instead of waiting for the rest of the class to catch. They can work on one big project incrementally, or on a series of smaller projects. Such projects should be designed to meet goals written in the student's gifted IEP.

Problems in school

GIEP meetings exist in order to review the efficacy of the plan, not the student. Accordingly, "The Plan fails the child; the child does not fail the plan." (McIntyre, 2004) Some students may have had a GIEP for years that has not met their needs. If a student is in danger of failing in any subject or in school, the GIEP meeting should be reconvened. GIEP team members discuss the problem, appraise the circumstances, discuss available alternatives, and arrive at a solution for the individual student, changing the GIEP accordingly. The team can even write a provision into the GIEP for problems, specifying that if the student is potentially failing a subject, is unlikely to meet a GIEP goal(s), or his/her performance becomes substantially worse, the GIEP team will reconvene, including the teacher of the subject involved, and the GIEP will be modified to address the problem(s).

Pre-testing

Gifted students often have mastered the content of a lesson or subject at their grade level before teaching has begun in that class. Making them sit through instruction in material they already know only bores and/or frustrates them and damages damaging their motivation;

- 36 -

moreover, they are prevented from learning new things in the subject at a higher level and at their own pace. The first section of the gifted IEP (GIEP) specifies the student's resent Levels of Educational Performance. When the GIEP team determines these, they can determine the need for pre-testing. Students whose pre-tests demonstrate mastery of material can be given alternate assignments that challenge them and allow them to learn new material. Students whose pre-tests demonstrate they have almost mastered a subject can be given only the parts they have not mastered to study, thereby saving time and redundancy. These students can use the rest of their class time for independent work on alternative assignments.

Acceleration

Acceleration is considered a more serious choice than other forms of accommodations for gifted students. Considerations for the student include the student's levels of emotional and social maturity, which can cause adjustment difficulties if a student is placed in chronologically older classes and is emotionally and/or socially unprepared. Historically, students skipped whole grades. While some cases still warrant such practices, students also can accelerate in individual subjects according to their levels of ability and performance. They can even work across grades if their learning levels dictate "straddling" two grade levels. Though accelerating is not always best, research finds gifted students more often benefit from ability-appropriate materials. Objective data on the student's current performance and potential are important to decisions to accelerate. Many school districts frown on acceleration, but they cannot have a policy prohibiting it. Attitudes against acceleration should be challenged acceleration represents the only way to benefit the student.

Purpose and nature of the gifted IEP (GIEP) relative to the nature of the gifted student's learning style and needs

The main purpose of the GIEP is to address the needs of the individual gifted student. By definition, a gifted student learns differently enough from others that standard teaching methods and curricula are unsuitable. The different nature of the gifted student's learning and needs is the reason for a GIEP. The nature of the GIEP is not a class(es) or program(s) in which the gifted student participates. Instead, the GIEP offers a plan for the student's education. As such, the GIEP must be monitored: the student's educational needs will evolve/change over time, and the plan then must be adapted to continue meeting them. If problems persist after modifying a GIEP, the team should revisit the student's Present Levels of Educational Performance, ascertain what additional assessment data and other information are needed, and develop a new, more suitable/effective GIEP. Teams should obtain outside expert consultations if needed.

Homework as a recurrent issue

Gifted children commonly start out in regular classes. Even after identification as gifted, the majority of gifted students are in regular classes most of the time with a small portion in supplementary gifted services like pull-out programs. They can end up with twice the homework: regular class assignments, plus gifted education assignments. Even students receiving accommodations in regular classrooms can receive double homework unless specific accommodations substitute gifted for regular homework. Having doubled work feels punishing, making students resent being identified as gifted. The excess can mean not doing all homework, damaging grades. Solutions include assigning more advanced work taking the same time but applying lesson knowledge instead of repeating it, which gifted students often do not need. For example, a student could do ten advanced math problems instead of 100 rote problems. Instead of writing simple sentences including spelling words, a student could write a poem or short story using them.

Determining eligibility for gifted educational services in public schools vs. services to disabled students

A major difference between determining eligibility for special services to disabled students versus special services to gifted students is that federal laws, such as IDEA 2004 and Section 500 of the Americans with Disabilities Act, specifically provide for special services to students with disabilities. The IDEA contains 13 categories of specific disabilities that qualify for special education services. Each covered disability has criteria to meet for a positive diagnosis. Section 500 of the ADA has a general definition of disability, and any student whose condition interferes with education according to that definition is eligible for services. However, the federal laws do not address giftedness as they do disabilities. Each state Department of Education decides how to address giftedness. Most departments begin with their definition of "gifted" to create rules. Local school districts comply with state eligibility rules. Some districts assign each school a gifted eligibility team to administer eligibility procedures.

Timely homework completion by gifted students

Problems result when gifted students are given both general and gifted education homework, thus doubling their load.

When such doubling is not the case, some gifted students still can have time management issues with homework. Here are some factors to consider: many gifted students are perfectionists. As such, they can expend excessive, unnecessary time trying to perfect their homework. Also, while some gifted students process information faster than non-gifted students, many do not. In fact, researchers have found that measures of working memory and processing speed on standardized IQ tests are poor indicators of giftedness. Timely homework completion is a skill that develops over time. If problems have developed over time, such problems also are resolved over time. These problems are addressed in the Specially Designed Instruction section of the GIEP. While teachers or local school districts may require homework completion to pass a course, many State Departments of Education do not.

Content skills vs. process skills

Content skills involve acquiring and retaining the information presented in a specific instructional subject area. Examples include learning the correct spelling of words; knowing the correct meaning of vocabulary words; knowing factual material such as places, names, and dates in history or social studies; remembering mathematical equations or formulas, etc. In contrast, process skills involve more interpretation of information. For example, a student not only knows what reportedly happened in a historical event, but s/he also can interpret that event in terms of its historical context, such as the frame of reference and viewpoints affecting participants. Process skills include analyzing information through comparisons-contrasts; generalizations; finding cause-and-effect relationships; classifying and sequencing; summarizing; and drawing inferences, conclusions, and

- 38 -

predictions. Such skills include applying critical thinking skills and systematic methods of inquiry, especially in sciences. Content and process skills are related because content must be learned to process it. Integrating the two is most effective.

Enrichment activities

Many gifted children have stronger reasoning abilities than do other students, and gifted children are better able to understand abstract concepts at earlier ages. Also, they often do not need to reinforce what they have learned with as much repetition as other children need. They should not simply be asked to recite or repeat something they have learned. Instead, they should be asked to use the higher cognitive skills they possess. For example, for comparison-contrast, you can ask the child the similarities and differences in words, familiar people, characters in a story, familiar songs, holidays, seasons of the year, birds and butterflies, etc. For categorizing, ask the child to group things, e.g. books, foods, toys, clothes, friends, or feelings. For sequencing, ask the child what happened in the beginning, middle, and end of a story. For summarizing, ask the child the most important events during a party, trip, or other activity with varied experiences.

Forming and testing hypotheses

Gifted children typically exhibit advanced abilities in conceptual thinking. Their skills should be developed with activities wherein they manipulate information rather than merely memorizing or recognizing it. To stimulate and practice hypothesizing, you can ask questions of a gifted child beginning with "What would happen if we...?" For example, what if we put a block into a glass filled with water? What if we put a glass over a lit candle? If we put tennis balls into a shoebox, how

many could it hold?, etc. Then you can test these hypotheses by following through and performing the hypothetical action to see what happens. These activities suit children in Piaget's Concrete Operations stage. For children who can think abstractly without concrete objects, activities can be extended to imaginary events and fantasies, e.g. "What would happen if you could fly?...if you were invisible?...if snow were ice cream?...if you were twelve feet tall?", etc.

Language experience stories

Younger gifted children with advanced abilities in language often will enjoy activities using language experience stories. You ask the child to make up a story on any subject the child prefers. For example, the story can be about the child's pet; the child's best friend or circle of friends; a favorite relative; a trip they took on vacation that they especially enjoyed; a day trip to a museum, zoo, planetarium; a party they had or attended; or any other subject of the child's choice. The child tells the story aloud and you write it down. You have the child draw illustrations to accompany the story. You then read the story back to the child, aloud from the printed version. Record your reading. Play back the recording and listen together, having the child follow the printed words to associate spoken and written language. Make multiple stories into a book for the child.

Making inferences in math and reading/reading readiness/language skills

One way young gifted children can be encouraged to exercise their cognitive abilities is through inferences, which require them to move beyond literal and concrete perceptions to more abstract thinking involving speculation based on existing information. For example, you can show a child a picture of people wearing uniforms and ask what their jobs may be, or show a picture of people with various facial expressions and ask what they might be feeling. In both cases, ask what could have happened before and after what is in the picture. For children with mathematical gifts, it is important to incorporate fun, game-like math activities into daily living routines. For developing reading readiness skills in young gifted children, you can label common household objects with their printed names on 3x5 cards. Start open-ended stories; let them make predictions and hypotheses about what will happen next and what will happen if that occurs.

General attitudes of most educators toward academic acceleration

The majority of research studies show that academic acceleration for gifted students affords them many benefits in both academic and social domains. However, despite these positive findings, most educators are reluctant to adopt or even consider acceleration as an option for fear that acceleration will result in problems in the students' emotional and social development. In contrast, educators who specialize in the education of the gifted student, and teachers and parents who have had personal experience with the acceleration of gifted students tend to have much more positive attitudes about accelerating and are more willing to select this option when a gifted student's profile indicates it. Pushing a student to accelerate can cause problems, as can accelerating an emotionally immature student or one continually getting negative responses from peers or educators. Having a small support group of similarly accelerated students eases the acceleration process.

Candidate for acceleration

If a student's scores on standardized achievement tests are many grades above age/grade level, or are so high that they are off the tests' charts, the student is a candidate for acceleration. If a formerly enthusiastic student begins exhibiting boredom and/or behavioral problems not due to other factors, this is another criterion. The student, parents, and school personnel ideally should all agree that accelerating would benefit the student. Early in the process, the IEP team and school psychologist should be involved. Classroom teachers should be consulted, as well as others who know the student best, e.g. the school's gifted and talented coordinator, principal, and/or guidance counselor. The school psychologist should evaluate the student relative to acceleration. Parents can consult state Department of Education coordinators of gifted education. Support from involved teachers and coordination and continuity from school officials is important. Acceleration decisions are usually made by the principal and/or IEP team/committee.

Positive effects of acceleration

Although acceleration must be decided for each individual student, research finds many benefits of acceleration for gifted students. Those students who exhibit advancement for their age far beyond their grade can even develop poor study habits, behavioral problems, become bored and daydream in school, or avoid attending school if they are forced to stay with their age-grade level. Especially in math, science, and English, some gifted students are more gifted than in other subjects. Such students may attend class with higher grades in their most gifted subject(s), but stay with their age's grade level for other subjects. Another form of acceleration is tutoring, either individually or in small groups. Some high

- 40 -

school students gifted in math, for example, might be in their school for all other subjects, but a group of them would attend advanced math classes with a local university's math professor a couple of days each week.

Concerns about acceleration

For those who worry that accelerating a gifted student will cause academic harm, they should be reassured that the majority of research shows that accelerated students get higher grades than gifted children who are not accelerated. Also, their grades compare positively with grades of the older students in the class. Researchers find that gifted students who accelerate report greater enthusiasm for and an interest in school as well. Another academic concern is that students who skip grades in a subject or skip whole grades will have gaps in their knowledge. This does occur, but less often than people think, because regular curricula contain so much redundancy. Gaps also do not present substantial problems for gifted children as they learn more quickly and thoroughly and can catch up more easily. Accelerating gifted students should not be penalized for unfamiliarity with any missed material, but should be allowed to cover it.

The most common worry of parents and educators about accelerating a gifted student to a higher grade is the impact it might have on the student's emotional and social development and wellbeing. They fear that while the child's intellectual development is undoubtedly at the higher grade level, his or her social and emotional development might lack the same levels of advancement. They worry about the child interacting with older children. However, researchers find children who are emotionally well-adjusted and socially comfortable before acceleration will report after accelerating

that they have two circles of friendships: one from their newer class of older students, and another from their previous age-level class and/or other children their age, with whom they maintain friendships. While gifted children who have trouble making friends may experience difficulty in older classes, many gifted students prefer friendships with older children, finding more in common with them due to their advanced development in many areas.

Accelerating in a single subject

Many gifted students in regular classes at their age level perceive that they are the smartest student in their class. When they are far enough beyond grade level to accelerate, the student often finds after acceleration that they are not the smartest in the group anymore. This change in status can require considerable adjustment, especially for students who have become accustomed to everything being too easy for them. In this situation, parents and teachers should not pressure students trying to adjust to unfamiliar circumstances. They should give them emotional support rather than pushing too much too soon for academic performance. They should also make clear to the student that a choice to accelerate can always be reversed if it seems unsuitable emotionally, socially, and/or academically for them. Adults should also help gifted students understand that reversing acceleration does not represent a failure on the part of the student.

On one hand, many educators are more receptive to accelerating a gifted student in one subject because the student learns the remaining majority of subjects with age-level classmates. These educators often feel this type of acceleration can avoid social and/or emotional problems for the student. On the other hand, certain factors must be considered when a gifted student is accelerating in only one subject. One is continuity. If educators do not carefully coordinate the student's programming, the student could learn accelerated materials one year, only to repeat these the following year. Teachers and curriculum specialists can help by defining what is taught in each grade for each subject. Another consideration is that elementary school students might need to attend a junior high/middle school, junior high/middle school students a high school, and high school students a college course, to accelerate in one subject. Transportation can present worse problems than academic or social concerns.

Mathematic giftedness

Many school programs for mathematically gifted students are designed with the goal of moving them through the curriculum as rapidly as possible. However, this approach of fast advancement does not cultivate a student's interest or passion for math. Zaccaro (2008) finds this analogous to teaching aspiring musicians "all scales and no music." Students made to practice scales but never allowed to play music that moves them emotionally will not develop passion for it. Practicing the structural fundamentals is necessary for mastery, but these fundamentals should not be taught exclusively. The same is true of math; students need to be given opportunities to work with material they find exciting and wondrous. Students can experience how the earth's circumference was determined 2500 years ago using simple geometry, apply knowledge of the speed of light to realize that viewing stars is time-traveling to the distant past, calculate ship-to-shore distances using trigonometry, and so forth.

Instructional models that provide a basis for reading curriculum units used in researching effectiveness

Three instructional models are: Carol Ann Tomlinson's Differentiation of Instruction model, which focuses on varying teaching methods; Sandra N. Kaplan's Depth and Complexity model, which focuses on attributes of deeper understanding and more complex knowledge; and Joseph S. Renzulli and Sally M. Reis' Schoolwide Enrichment Model (SEM), which uses educational enhancements that simultaneously benefit all students and address the special needs of gifted students. The National Research Center on Gifted and Talented (NRC/GT) has a longitudinal study basing curricula on these instructional models. By sampling school districts nationwide that implement gifted and talented programs, these studies' findings represent diverse populations, socioeconomic levels, and urban, suburban, and rural settings. These sample schools are selected from nominations by educators who develop curriculum models; state gifted education directors; and representatives from state and national organizations. Outcomes are measured by (1) state standards extended for advanced reading and math achievement; and (2) performance-based measures of investigative and problem-solving skills.

Research questions related to curricula

Some research teams, including teams on a nationwide level, are interested in examining comparisons of different criteria for identifying gifted students, the effects of such criteria on assessment results and on under-represented populations, and comparisons of the effects of general education curricula and model-based curricula on gifted students. They ask research questions such as:

When comparing standardized and performance-based measures of reading and math, whether the criteria for identifying giftedness interact in any ways with the type of instructional method (i.e. general education curricula vs. theoretical model-based curricula) delivered. They want to discover if students not identified as gifted are helped or harmed in achievement by model-based curricula, and if non-identified students in their non-treatment and treatment classes perform the same or differently on standardized reading and math achievement tests. These researchers are also interested in how teacher implementations of model-based curricula are affected by personal and environmental variables.

Environmental and personal variables that influence the way teachers implement curricula

A number of factors in the environment and within the individual teacher can influence the way teachers implement curriculum units in reading and math. While curriculum units based on theoretical models adhere to principles of the applicable model, their implementation can vary as it is shaped by personal and environmental variables. For example, the grade level of students being taught will make a difference in the way that teachers implement curriculum. The school subject and department also will influence what elements are emphasized or minimized. Even the school building can make a difference in how teachers carry out their curricula. Variables at the school district level also affect teachers' understanding of a curriculum and how they implement it. Teachers' personal variables include their duration of classroom experience, their beliefs about learning and teaching, their particular approach to classroom management, and the grade level(s) and subject(s) they teach.

Benefits to school districts for participating in research studies

Research studies regarding effective teaching methods in gifted education often develop curriculum units to test in actual practice at schools. Such units are designed to challenge gifted students, differentiated for all student levels in general education classrooms and based upon national standards. Such units educationally benefit more students at more levels than non-differentiated instruction. Participating school districts often receive tools for the identification and the assessment of gifted students free of charge, which represents a financial benefit. Major research centers also provide support for educators' professional development, benefiting school districts financially and benefiting teachers, other school personnel, and students. This support often includes online technical assistance, an additional benefit addressing the increasing use of online resources and tools. Participation in a research study conducted by a center offering professional development courses for educators also gives priority to some members of school district staffs in registering for these courses.

Qualitative research vs. quantitative research

Quantitative research methods use statistical procedures to measure or quantify phenomena in giftedness and gifted education, while qualitative research methods do not use such measures. Qualitative research is interpretive in nature. Implicit in the qualitative approach is the assumption that one must investigate giftedness as a whole in order to understand it. Quantitative research typically analyzes components of giftedness/gifted education. Proponents of qualitative research argue that such piecemeal examinations overlook important parts of the holistic appreciation they advocate. Rather than an absolute reality posited in quantitative research, qualitative methods propose multiple realities, which themselves vary across different times and places. Holistic understanding of the complexity, richness, and depth of giftedness/gifted education often reveals meanings that help researchers gain new insights. While all quantitative research is conducted according to an overall structure, qualitative research methods vary in their individual theoretical orientations relative to the specific topic or phenomenon under study.

One kind of qualitative research is grounded theory. In this approach, a theory is developed inductively (rather than deductively, which uses the reverse process of formulating a hypothesis and then collecting data to test it) from a body of data. While simpler quantitative statistical tests such as analysis of variance yield only the main effects of one variable upon another, grounded theory takes a case-oriented rather than a variable-oriented approach, assuming that variables interact in more complex ways and function as a whole within a case. Grounded theory also has a comparative orientation, based on John Stuart Mill's methods of similarities and differences, to uncover the causes. Another type of qualitative research is historical. The researcher collects data about past events, and objectively evaluates these events to test his/her hypotheses about their trends, causes, and/or effects, which can help to explain current related events and predict future related ones.

One type of qualitative research is the case study. This method seeks to gain insights into a phenomenon such as giftedness by studying one individual case of the phenomenon in great depth and detail. The case could be an individual gifted student, a specific class of gifted students, a school for gifted students, or a particular event involving gifted students. Phenomenology is another type of qualitative research. Phenomenology refers to the process wherein the researcher describes the structures of his or her experiences as they are apprehended by the researcher's consciousness, without using theories, assumptions taken from other fields/disciplines, or deductive reasoning to influence that description. Another kind of qualitative research is represented by ethnography. In ethnography, the researcher makes detailed field observations of sociocultural events or characteristics, typically within a particular community or population. This type of research can lend itself to studying groups of gifted students and gifted educational programs.

Curriculum units with differentiated instruction for "academically diverse" students

Some research groups interested in determining which methods of identification, testing, curriculum, and instruction are most effective for gifted students develop curriculum units to use in their studies. They then compare test scores of students taught using different curricula. Some researcher-developed curriculum units feature differentiated instruction in order to tailor teaching to the individual needs of "academically diverse students." These units place emphasis on problem-solving skills, conceptual thinking, and "real-world disciplinary inquiry" (e.g. using the scientific method to investigate subjects in various fields applied to real life). Curriculum units also function as tools for assessing individual students' learning needs. In addition, they help students attain progressively higher levels of expertise. Researchers believe that their work will foster both fairness and achievement in school systems nationwide and will nurture student gifts by focusing on gifted identification, model-based math and reading curriculum units, and traditional and performance-based assessments.

Collecting and analyzing data used in qualitative research

Qualitative research is descriptive, experiential, and interpretive rather than statistical or numerical, as is quantitative research. Qualitative research demands rich, detailed descriptions to reveal the research process and to communicate implicit knowledge. As such, qualitative research uses three methods of data collection and analysis: observations, interviews, and self-reports. In observation, the researcher observes the nonverbal and verbal behaviors of study subjects (avoiding influencing the subjects' behavior insofar as is possible) and records descriptions of observed behaviors. Interviews are interactive with the subjects: the researchers first ask the participants to describe specified events or phenomena orally, and then the researcher records the participants' responses. Researchers also may ask participants to write down descriptions of their experiences; these are self-reports. Researchers analyze the initial data they collect to inform and direct further data collection. All these methods can be used to obtain data from gifted students, their parents, teachers, non-gifted peers, etc.

Advantages and disadvantages of qualitative research

Because quantitative forms of research using statistical analysis are the predominant methods used in educational and psychological research as well as in other social sciences, critics of qualitative types of research often regard these methods as more subjective. However, as Myers (2002) states, "Since we maintain our humanity throughout the research process, it is largely impossible to escape the subjective experience..." This humanity includes intuitive realizations and "aha moments." Qualitative research demands extensive time and effort. Furthermore, because of the subjective nature of qualitative research results, these results obtained with samples cannot be generalized to larger populations in the same manner as can the results from statistical studies. However, Myers and other researchers (e.g. Neill, 2006) find qualitative methods to transcend those drawbacks with other redeeming qualities, such as in-depth descriptions with sufficient detail for readers to realize the idiosyncrasies of the individual research situation, and providing the researcher's perspective on that situation.

Qualitative methodologies tend to be inductive, i.e. they proceed from the specific to the general and generate new theories. Quantitative methods tend to be deductive, i.e. they proceed from the general to the specific and test existing theories. Qualitative methods incorporate more subjective aspects, while quantitative methods restrict findings to objective facts and figures. For example, if you wanted to find out which of two curricula is preferred by individual gifted students in a general classroom, you likely would use qualitative methodology and ask students which curricula they liked better—thus introducing a subjective element. If you wanted to find out which curriculum resulted in higher scores on standardized achievement tests taken by the gifted students in the general classroom, you likely would use quantitative methodology to determine differences in test scores and to discover whether a correlational or causal relationship (or both) exists between the curricula and the test scores.

For educators who want to determine the grade level at which a gifted student is reading, for example, quantitative methods are best for measurements that can be represented numerically and somewhat discretely. If a gifted child in a regular second grade is tested as reading at a sixth-grade level, this finding helps teachers select reading material for that child that is intellectually more suitable, yet still age-appropriate emotionally, socially, and experientially. Quantitative measures are used in standardized tests of IQ, knowledge, and academic achievement. Qualitative methods are more helpful for determining which content areas are an individual gifted student's favorites. Such methods also are useful for discovering a gifted student's particular learning style as well as the student's academic strengths and learning needs. Qualitative data collection methods such as interviews, observations, and self-reports can yield thorough profiles of each gifted student as a whole person, incorporating intellectual, psychological, emotional, social, and behavioral characteristics.

Investigating teaching methods, identifying the terms random sampling, independent variable, dependent variable, manipulate, and control group

Introduce two teaching methods, neither one normally used with the students. Divide students into two experimental groups and one control group by random sampling; i.e. they all have an equal chance of being in any group, preventing biased selection. One experimental group gets a lecture on a new topic followed by a question-and-answer/discussion session; the other gets a hands-on activity on the same topic followed by a question-and-answer/discussion session. The control group contains comparable students receiving no treatment; e.g., they receive the same teaching method normally used in your school, on the same topic as the experimental groups. The control group helps rule out the influences of extraneous/confounding variables on differing results between experimental groups, supporting the experimental treatments' differing influences. All groups receive the same pre-test and post-test on the topic. The teaching method is the independent variable, which was manipulated. The dependent variable is post-test score.

Respective natures and characteristics of qualitative and quantitative methods

Popular conceptions of research methodologies characterize quantitative methods as using hard data, numbers, objective information, and findings that can be generalized to the larger populations represented by study samples; and qualitative methods as using "soft" data, words, subjective impressions, and findings more specific to the study's subjects but not generalizable to larger groups. Each method has its own strengths and weaknesses. Rather than choosing one or another method by personal preference, many researchers (cf. Neill, 2006), believe the nature of the research question should dictate the most applicable methodology. Neill also points out that qualitative and quantitative methods are not opposing paradigms; rather, each has its use, and the existence of mixed-methods studies proves they can be used together. Researchers are more likely to use qualitative methods earlier in a study to learn more comprehensively about a topic, using quantitative methods later on to seek precise answers to more specific questions.

Three main quantitative research designs

One quantitative research design is descriptive, which seeks to obtain more information about a specific attribute or phenomenon within a field. Descriptive designs can be used to defend existing practices, identify problems, develop theories, develop opinions, or identify others' work in the same field. Descriptive designs do not look for causal relationships or manipulate variables. Experimental designs represent the paradigm for using the scientific method. As such, main elements of experimental designs are randomization, manipulation, and control. Experimenters randomly select participants, i.e. each has an equal chance of selection. Experimenters manipulate some variable(s) in the study, and some participants receive some kind of intervention/treatment. Experimenters also control some variables. A common form of experimental design is the before/after or pre-test/post-test design. Quasi-experimental designs are used when control is unfeasible and/or to protect validity when randomization, manipulation, or control is missing. Correlational/ex post facto designs look for relationships (NOT causality) without manipulating variables.

Mean, median, and mode as used in quantitative research designs

Statistically, mean, median, and mode are measures of central tendency, meaning they quantify trends wherein the majority of values fall near the center/middle. The mean/arithmetic mean is an average of all values obtained. For example, if in a group of 11 gifted students, four score 100% on a test, three score 96%, two score 94%, one scores 92%, and one scores 90%, the mean = 96%. If one student scored 70%, this would corrupt or skew the mean. The median represents the midpoint of all scores. In this example, with this distribution: 100+100+100+100+96+96+96+94+94+92+90, the midpoint is 96. Median does not inform the other values; if one student scored 70%, the median would not change. The mode is the most frequent value; in this example, 100. Mode does not reflect non-central, extreme values. If this example had four scores of 100% and four of 96%, it would have a bimodal distribution.

Bell curve and the meaning of normal distribution in statistical analysis

A bell curve, aka a normal curve or Gaussian curve, graphically visualizes a normal distribution. Most values obtained fall near the median (middle/center), and fewer fall higher or lower, resulting in a curve with a bell shape – higher in the center, sloping downward toward the edges, and symmetrical, with equal numbers above and below the middle. With normal distributions, the mean (average of all values), median (the middle of all values) and mode (the value occurring most often) should be equal or nearly so. If a standardized IQ test is administered to a general education class including a few gifted students and the scores are plotted on a graph, the overall distribution of all scores is likely to be normal; however, the few gifted students' scores are likely NOT to be found near the median with most other student scores, but at one extremity, among the fewest and highest values.

Percentages of values in a statistically normal distribution that fall within 1, 2, and 3 standard deviations from the mean

When data from a group can be graphed as a bell curve, they have normal distribution. The largest number of scores will fall on or around the mean or average. In normal distributions, approximately 68% of the values fall somewhere within 1 standard deviation above or below the mean; about 95% of the values fall within 2 standard deviations above or below the mean; and about 99% fall within 3 standard deviations above or below the mean. A steep curve with most values near the mean shows a small standard deviation; flatter curves show larger standard deviations with more values spread away from the mean. If the average IQ score in a regular classroom is 100, with one gifted student having a score of 150, that score represents 1% of the population, as it is more than 3 standard deviations (typically 15 points with IQ tests, x 3 = 45) above 100.

Standard deviation and variance

In statistics, standard deviation shows how much the numbers in a given set vary within their distribution and how close to or spread away they are from the mean/average. Standard deviation is the square root of variance. Variance is calculated by squaring each variation from the mean and averaging the squares. Standard deviation indicates how much variation around the average is expected; greater variations are statistically significant. In IQ scores, the most common standard deviation is 15 points; variations of + 2 standard deviations, i.e. 30 points above or below the mean, are statistically significant. Thus, a student scoring 134 does not necessarily have a higher IQ than one scoring 130 on the same IQ test. However, a student scoring 160 compared to another scoring 130 on the same test shows a significant difference of 30 points, or two standard deviations. This difference is sometimes used for labeling levels or degrees of giftedness.

Reliability, validity, internal validity and external validity

In scientific research, reliability refers to whether a measurement can be repeated with consistent results, regardless of the administrator. For example, a reliable standardized achievement test given to the same gifted student should yield similar scores each time, even when different teachers/personnel administer the assessment. Validity refers to whether an instrument or procedure measures what it claims to measure. For example, a standardized achievement test is not a valid instrument for measuring IQ; conversely, a standardized IQ test is not a valid instrument for measuring academic performance. Internal validity refers to whether the findings of an experimental study are attributable to the intervention or treatment used in the study and not to any other variables. For example, students could test better due to being taught a different curriculum or to having a different teacher. External validity refers how much a study's findings can be generalized to populations beyond the study's sample.

Mathematic challenge and frustration

Many mathematically gifted students enjoy challenges that engage their superior abilities for calculating and solving problems. However, gifted students who only have experience with effortless school work become uncomfortable confronting challenges and/or frustration inherent in learning more difficult material. In addition to teaching advanced students, teachers are charged with the job of helping them realize that confining their education to easy pursuits deprives them of many rewards, and a life without struggle leads to less achievement and fulfillment. Teachers can give students examples illustrating challenges to adults. One educator (Zaccaro, 2008) would tell his students about the time he did not calculate whether his rope was long enough to rappel off a cliff and reach the ground, and he had to jump 15 feet. He also gave them problems to work where mistakes were common so they could see that making errors was not the end of the world.

Connecting math and science to real life

Since math and science are so often heavy in calculations and facts, students are usually not taught how these subjects relate to the real world. All students, especially gifted students, need to find meaning in an academic subject and understand how it applies in life. We may not appreciate enough that math and science are not like people whose opinions we can disagree with; they provide hard, objective, unchangeable facts. Teachers can show students the consequences of ignoring facts with examples like these: mathematicians and engineers advised not launching the Challenger space shuttle, but management overruled them, thereby leading to the deadly explosion. Pop singer Aaliya died in a plane crash after pilot and crew ignored the mathematics indicating airplane overload and flew regardless. A mathematician proved racial bias in jury selection by calculating that the mathematical probability of fair selection was approximately 1 in 1,000,000,000,000,000.

Recognition and reinforcement

Student musicians perform in concerts and receive applause from crowds of schoolmates and parents. Student athletes compete in games or meets, also attended by cheering crowds. In addition to internal motivations to use their talents, these students obtain powerful external reinforcement from this positive public attention. In contrast, students with mathematical and scientific gifts do not enjoy the same opportunities to show their skills regularly in such public arenas. Students gifted in academic subjects do not experience much formal recognition for their abilities outside of good school grades and teacher approval. However, such students also need to receive positive reinforcement in order for them to appreciate the great value of their gifts. They may also need to receive validation for their accomplishments, as some students may attribute their successes to their natural gifts and mistakenly feel that they have not added any effort to developing them.

When motivation for particular subjects may be at odds with actual talent

Some students are gifted in certain areas, yet their interests lay elsewhere, where they are less talented and even exhibit weaknesses. For example, a parent and retired educator had a gifted child with talent in mathematics and playing violin. However, his passions were for soccer and singing, where he was not gifted or average, but comparatively weak. His parents did not press him to focus on his gifted areas or give up on what he loved because he did not excel. Despite shortcomings in favored fields, his passion and persistence eventually won him a place on his high school soccer team and he realized his goal of making All-State choir in senior year. He teaches and directs voice and coaches soccer as an adult, happy with his choices. This illustrates that gifted students need not confine their efforts to gifted areas and may succeed in other fields with passion and perseverance.

Mathematical word problems that that a teacher can give to allow challenges appropriate to different ability levels

1. First level: A gas tank was ¼ full. You add eight gallons and it is now ¾ full. How many gallons does this tank hold?
2. Second level: Sound travels one mile in 5 seconds. You yell near a rock wall and hear the echo 20 seconds later. How far are you from the wall?

3. Third level: A sprinkler throws water in a circle 15 feet away. It is in the center of a lawn 30 x 30 feet. How many square feet does the sprinkler miss?
4. Highest level – *Teachers can present class awards to students solving these problems for positive reinforcement, teaching them to appreciate their gifts, building self-esteem, and enhancing motivation*: Alice, Barbara, Charlotte, and Deborah are sisters inheriting money from an aunt. Alice got ½ the money. Barbara got ¼. Charlotte got ⅛. Deborah got the rest, which equaled $1,750.00. What total amount did all four sisters receive?

Motivational tools teachers can use to enhance math and science

Students gifted in certain fields such as music and sports, enjoy positive reinforcement received for performing in public arenas like musical concerts and athletic events where large groups of people, many of whom they know as fellow students and parents, applaud and cheer them. Students with gifts in math and science do not have the same opportunities for official public recognition. Educator Ed Zaccaro (2008) recommends "Einstein Awards." He designated very difficult math/science problems as "Einstein problems." When students solved one, he presented them in class with an award featuring a picture of Einstein. He reported dramatic responses from students: One parent told Zaccaro that his daughter said the award was the best thing that had ever happened to her. Another said she had to restrict her son to two hours of math per night as he always wanted to solve more Einstein problems. Simple positive reinforcement is a powerful motivator.

Learning characteristic of elementary school students gifted in math

Often children with mathematical gifts can grasp new concepts very quickly. In the general education classroom, they end up without recourse to additional intellectual exercise while they wait for the rest of the students to understand and master the new math ideas presented. Some consequences of letting gifted students go unchallenged are boredom, less than optimal thinking skills, and undesirable study habits. One way to offer them challenges is through differentiated instruction. The teacher can present math problems with graduated levels of difficulty and complexity. When students have a choice of problems at different levels, they have the opportunity to try to solve problems just within their current cognitive capacity. Such methodology challenges students with problems that are not too easy, without overly frustrating them by being out of range of their ability; it cultivates their passion for math; and it stimulates their cognitive growth and development.

Educational inclusion

In recent years, the federal government has passed legislation guaranteeing students with disabilities a free, appropriate public education, including special education services as needed to accommodate disabilities in order to provide this education. This legislation has led to great emphasis on inclusion in education. However, the laws do not address students with gifts. Educators still apply the notion of inclusion to gifted students in that they should experience working with non-gifted students. This is true, but it is not a big concern as most gifted students in public schools are in regular classrooms most or all of the time. Equally important is the need for gifted students to be able to work with similarly gifted students. Such collaborative work not only promotes their cognitive development. It also contributes to their emotional and social development through sharing ideas, debates, and constructive disagreements and through decreasing the social isolation that many math-gifted children often experience.

Single-subject acceleration plan in math

For a first-grader able to learn third-grade math, the school's single-subject acceleration plan could include the following provisions: The first- and third-grade teachers will schedule math at the same times. The third-grade teacher is the teacher of record for math. The student is not required to do any first-grade math assignments. A school staff member assigned to monitor the plan meets weekly with the student to assess her success and satisfaction and weekly with the third-grade teacher to discuss any areas of difficulty for the student. Throughout the transitional period, the student's parents are lent copies of the first-, second-, and third-grade math textbooks so they can help her at home with studying and homework. Until she can make new friends in the third-grade class, the student is assigned to sit next to a student in the third-grade class who is her friend and her next-door neighbor at home.

Single-subject acceleration plan in science

For a fifth-grader accelerating to sixth-grade science, the plan can provide: The fifth-grade teacher and/or gifted intervention specialist will find/create curriculum that compacts assessments on fifth-grade science standards unfamiliar to the student, which she completes in free time at school and/or home with parental help. The staff person assigned as monitor meets weekly with the sixth-grade teacher to discuss student progress

and weekly with the student to discuss her adjustment throughout the transition. The student uses the elementary school's webcam/Skype/similar software for virtual attendance to sixth-grade science class at the middle school. The technology coordinator gives student and teachers a short tutorial to facilitate this. After transition, to assure ongoing progress, dual-credit courses in 7th and 8th grade are arranged so after one high-school semester, the student becomes a sophomore eligible to take state graduation tests that spring. High school credit is awarded for completing 9th-grade science in 8th grade.

Skipping grades

If the school has determined a gifted first-grader can do third-grade work, the written whole-grade acceleration plan should include such provisions as these: The third-grade teacher should report and discuss any signs of academic and/or emotional stress in the student to the school staff person assigned to monitor plan implementation. The monitor should check with the third-grade teacher weekly on student progress. A gifted intervention specialist and/or third-grade teacher should obtain/develop curricula and assessments that compact only the second-grade standard the student has never experienced to make up anything he will miss by skipping second grade. He will complete these standards/skills during free time at school and/or home with his parents helping him as needed to master them. Upon successful transition, he remains in the accelerated grade until additional acceleration options are indicated. By middle school, the student's program should be reviewed to see if dual-enrollment options might benefit him.

Assuring continuing progress after the transition phase

For a gifted first-grader placed in a third-grade class for math who has successfully completed the transition phase, the section of the school's plan to support her continuing progress could include provisions for the following strategies: In fourth grade, arrange for her to take an online math course at the sixth-grade level, and another at the seventh-grade level when she is in fifth grade. The plan can incorporate an option for her to complete an Introductory Algebra course when she is in seventh grade, or sooner if she is ready for it. Satisfactorily completing the online courses and Algebra/other educational options in the plan will be treated as the equivalents of completing traditional courses as prerequisites for enrollment in advanced high school-level math courses. The plan can provide that the student receives high school credits for completing Algebra and other high school math courses while she is in middle school.

Rules that a school district's testing policy might include for gifted students accelerating in one subject

In some districts, rules differ for a student's first and subsequent years of subject acceleration. In the first year, if a test exists at the accelerated-subject grade level, testing is required for students whose overall/age-level grade is third-grade or higher; whose accelerated-subject grade-level is fourth-grade or higher; and the accelerated subject is reading or math. Testing is more likely optional if the accelerated subject is science, social studies, or writing; and if the student's overall level is second-grade or lower and the accelerated subject is third-grade or higher. If no test exists at the accelerated grade level and one exists at the student's overall grade level, testing may be optional. In subsequent years of acceleration, if a test exists at the accelerated grade level, testing is usually required. If no test exists at the accelerated-subject grade level and one exists at the student's overall grade level, districts may prohibit testing.

Acceleration in social studies from intermediate to high school classes

Some state Departments of Education (New York, for example) allow gifted eighth-grade students to accelerate in social studies for high school diploma credit if the superintendent or designee ascertains the student's readiness. Eighth-grade students can be awarded this credit by the high school if they attend the high school with high-school students and pass the course with the same requirements as the high-school students. Alternatively, an eighth-grade student can gain high-school credit by passing the state proficiency or Regents examination, and the credit is accepted as a transfer credit by any high school in the same state. If the state has no proficiency examination or similar assessment in social studies, an eighth-grade student can pass a course in his or her middle/junior high/intermediate school that is approved for high school credit by that district's superintendent or designee. Local examinations indicating school principal-determined high school-level performance may also be used.

High quality of gifted classroom instruction

To be of sufficiently high quality, classroom instruction for gifted students should accomplish the following:
(1) It should adapt, modify, or differentiate the grade-level curriculum and teaching practices to address the special educational needs of gifted students;
(2) It should give gifted students ways in which they can show their

proficiency in the required curriculum, and thereafter give them educational opportunities that present them with appropriate challenges;

(3) It should be made up of curriculum options, resource materials, and teaching approaches that are differentiated and reside along a continuum;

(4) It should allow for flexibility in educational arrangements for gifted students, to include such options as the use of compacted material for accelerating or advanced students; subject and/or whole-grade acceleration; independent study agreements and research projects; and

(5) It should be designed with the goal of increasing the depth and breadth of knowledge that learners with high ability acquire.

Curriculum compacting

Compacting is a way to streamline regular curricula for gifted students who learn faster. Compacting also can fill instruction gaps for students accelerating to higher grades and for those using the time saved by compacting to pursue enrichment activities. Sequential steps in the curriculum compacting process include: identifying pertinent learning objectives for the subject or grade level; locating or creating pre-test instruments for these objectives; identifying student candidates for compacting; pre-testing these candidates to ascertain their learning levels of the identified objectives; get rid of teaching, drilling, and/or practicing time for students who have already mastered the objectives; for objectives students have not mastered, streamline their instruction for the gifted students' faster rates of mastery; offer options of enrichment or acceleration for students who have exhausted the regular curriculum; and maintain records of the

entire process and of instruction options available for students participating in compacted curricula.

Comprehension skills included in enriched social studies skills

In social studies, students should be able to attain and demonstrate the following: recognizing cause and effect relationships in social studies topics; making comparisons and contrasts among concepts presented in social studies; making connections between events, persons, things, etc.; evaluating the subject content in social studies; paraphrasing the social studies content they have learned and showing thorough understanding; differentiating between facts and opinions in social studies; drawing inferences from social studies material they learn; drawing conclusions about a topic in social studies; locating and solving social studies problems with multiple steps and ; managing and understanding various interpretations of social studies events or issues; and making decisions.

General goals of a good gifted education program

Good gifted education programs seek to facilitate the gifted student's mastery of basic reading and math skills at paces and depths suitable to the student's abilities; to foster abilities of reasoning and critical thinking; to create an environment conducive to divergent thought; to promote inquiry; to promote challenging attitudes relative to learning; to develop higher level skills in spoken and written language; to develop skills and methods for doing research; to cultivate students' comprehension of issues, problems, themes, and systems of knowledge that structure the extrinsic environment; to foster student development of self-understanding; to enable learning experiences outside of school that fit the

- 53 -

individual student's educational needs; to provide or improve opportunities for future student development and planning; to develop creative thinking and problem-solving skills; to foster effective social skills for interpersonal interaction and coping; and to develop the student's skills of metacognition for self-direction and independent learning.

Measuring creativity

Although many researchers agree about common elements of creativity such as the originality, applicability, and value to society of creative work, they find it much more difficult to agree about which methods to use to make their definitions operational, and about which instruments of measurement to use. Creativity is such a complex quality that most measures cannot sum it up alone. Experts advise using multiple measures, but even this tactic can fail to achieve a comprehensive representation. Forty years ago, researchers found that the absence of any one unified and broadly accepted theory of creativity caused problems with understanding creativity's relationship to other abilities, the ramifications of different testing instruments and administrations, and operational definitions. Researchers find the same problems today. Meanwhile, so many creativity tests have been developed with varying degrees of psychometric credibility that difficulties in focusing on criteria have only increased.

Aspects of creativity that measurement instruments can and cannot identify

Researchers find that many instruments designed to measure creativity can identify the characteristics of fluency in ideation and divergence in thought, commonly accepted as components of creativity. However, they find that these measures do not predict future creative behaviors in a student identified as

creative. Some scientists attribute this characteristic not to psychometrics but poor methodology—e.g. some studies were not continued long enough, data not having normal distributions did not receive adequate statistical procedures, or the criteria for outcomes in longitudinal studies were not well operationalized. Some researchers also note that while personal definitions and theories of creativity are not included, they should be. These researchers have proposed that individuals acting creatively are directed by their personal beliefs about the nature of creativity, how to nurture and measure creativity, and that these beliefs may differ substantially from the theories that experts in the study of creativity have developed.

Differences between intelligence and creativity measures

Traditionally, standardized intelligence tests were used to determine whether a student was gifted. IQ scores above certain numbers (e.g. above 120, 130, etc.) qualified a student as gifted. However, IQ scores are an indication of intellectual giftedness rather than of creativity. Traditional standardized intelligence tests typically feature questions or problems with only one right answer. When taking this kind of intelligence test, the student must use convergent thinking to narrow down the possibilities to the correct one. In contrast, many measures of creativity test divergent thinking, which generates multiple ideas and possible responses. During the 1960s, J. P. Guilford and E. P. Torrance both developed standardized tests of divergent thinking that are still popular today. Because the traditional standardized intelligence tests require convergent thinking and little or no divergent thinking, and because divergent thinking is identified as a key characteristic of creativity, scientists have come to hypothesize that intelligence and

- 54 -

creativity are separate constructs.

Guilford Battery of tests for creative thinking

Psychologist Joy Paul Guilford (1897-1987) formulated his Structure of the Intellect model in 1962, identifying 180 different kinds of thinking, many of them divergent. He found that the types of divergent thinking most pertinent to creativity were the abilities to generate new information from existing information and to transform knowledge or experience into new patterns and configurations. Based on this model, Guilford developed a battery of tests for creative thought. This battery's ten tests each measure divergence in producing the following: (1) Names for Stories - semantic units; (2) What to Do with It - semantic categories; (3) Similar Meanings - semantic relationships; (4) Writing Sentences - semantic systems; (5) Kinds of People - semantic implications; (6) Make Something Out of It - figural units; (7) Different Letter Groups - figural categories; (8) Making Objects - figural systems; (9) Hidden Letters - figural transformations; and (10) Adding Decorations - figural implications.

The Guilford Battery contains ten tests of different types of divergent thinking, a cognitive process associated with creativity. Half of the tests are verbal measures, and half are nonverbal/figural measures. The verbal measures portion of the battery asks students to offer as many solutions as they can in the following categories: names for stories, verbal classes/categories, synonyms, sentence structures, verbal inferences about categories, figures, categories of figures, systems of figures, transformations of figures, and inferences about the figures. Each test is timed and scored for fluency by number of responses and for originality by statistical infrequency of responses. Not much validity research exists regarding these tests. Follow-up studies by Meeker (1978) found that students identified as creative by Guilford's tests in elementary school also had high creativity scores in high school. Michael and Bachelor (1990) found limited confirmation of Guilford's findings through conducting factor analyses.

Torrance Tests of Creative Thinking

In order to operationalize creativity for research purposes, E.P. Torrance focused on its problem-solving aspect. His tests include nonverbal and verbal forms. "Thinking Creatively with Pictures" features three activity groups: namely, drawing lines elaborating on one shape, drawing lines finishing an incomplete picture, and drawing as many different pictures as possible using the same shape. "Thinking Creatively with Words" features six activities involving generating questions, alternate uses for things, and guesses. All these activities are timed and scored for fluency, flexibility, and originality. In addition, the nonverbal forms are scored for elaboration. Torrance's tests apply to grade levels from kindergarten through graduate school and are the most widely used creativity tests. They also have the most research supporting their validity worldwide, as they have been translated into many languages. While their longitudinal predictive validity is not high (.62 for males, .57 for females), Torrance indicates they match or exceed rates for intelligence measures.

Findings regarding the personality characteristics of persons with various creative gifts

Jane Piirto (Understanding Those Who Create, 1998) found that when compared to others with creative gifts, artists are more impulsive and spontaneous. The author found that writers tend more toward nonconformity than do the other creatively gifted types. In addition, Piirto found that in comparison to other creative types, musicians tend more toward introversion. She discovered that architects are not as flexible as other creative persons. Furthermore, she concluded that creative engineers and inventors were likely to be more well-adjusted overall than were other creative types. These findings imply that specific personality traits may need to be considered in order to make predictions, since different personality traits are associated with different domains of creativity. Kerr and Gagliardi (2009) find this domain-specific approach more useful than "…seeking one creative personality type that fits all creative occupations." Indeed, the latter seems doomed to failure in light of the many types of creativity.

Personality traits that researchers have associated with creativity

Some researchers view creativity as a strictly cognitive process; others view it as a group of personality traits. Kerr and Gagliardi (2009) assert that while some students might be identified as creative in their thinking, without personality characteristics such as independence and persistence, these students may not produce any creative work. Hence they recommend that both aspects be considered. Divergent thinking is the most prevalent cognitive attribute studied in creativity research. With respect to personality, creativity has been most associated with the traits of autonomy, introversion, and openness to experience. (The latter two traits are included in the "Big Five" personality traits identified by McCrae & Costa and others.) Researchers have noted (e.g. King and Pope 1999, Feist 1999) that creative types are likely to work independently on their creative products and to avoid much social stimulation and group influence. Openness to experience

affords the stimulation of new ideas, questions, and topics.

Acceleration, complexity, depth, challenge, and creativity

With acceleration, the master educational standard has fewer tasks assigned. Students are assessed prior to instruction. Acceleration clusters are determined by higher-order cognitive skills. With complexity, multiple higher-level thinking skills are used. Use of multiple resources is required. More variables are added to study. With depth, students study multiple applications of a concept they have learned. They might conduct original research into subjects they study, or they may develop an original product. With challenge, students make use of advanced resource materials or work with more sophisticated content in subjects they study. They can apply their learning across different academic disciplines. Furthermore, they are expected to be able to explain their process of reasoning to others. With creativity, students might design and/or build a model based upon principles and/or criteria they have learned. Alternatives for various academic tasks, products, and assessments are made available. Oral and written communication to the real-world audience is emphasized.

Research and writing skills that gifted students should have in enriched social studies courses

Gifted students should acquire and demonstrate a number of skills for doing research, writing up research results, and writing in general. Students should learn how to acquire the information they need. In addition, they should learn different note-taking practices, how to organize information, and be able to identify primary and secondary sources of research and know how to use them. They should be able to read textbooks with comprehension, and they should have/cultivate the ability to look for patterns in the material they read. They should also be able to interpret the information they encounter in social studies, and then analyze, synthesize, and apply the information to different circumstances and real-world situations. They should be able to support their viewpoints using pertinent documents and facts. They should learn to create bibliographies and webographies. Finally, they should recognize what is important in research and writing.

Enrichment skills in interpersonal interactions and group relationships

Social studies skills for gifted students that fall under the area of interpersonal and group relations skills include the following: students should learn to define social studies terms and identify fundamental assumptions made in social studies. They should learn how to identify the existence of conflicts between or among the values of the people and groups involved in social studies topics and issues. They should learn to recognize when and where stereotypes exist and to avoid being influenced by them. In addition, they also should learn how to avoid engaging in stereotypes, themselves. They should become able to acknowledge various points of view. Gifted students in social studies courses should develop empathy for and understanding of others. They should participate in group discussions and planning in their social studies classes. Finally, they should be able to collaborate in order to attain goals cooperatively and take responsibility for completing tasks.

Maps or globes, graphs, and images

Gifted students participating in enriched social studies courses need to learn how to read maps and read, understand, and apply map legends, scales of miles, and mapping symbols. They need to be able to read and use compass roses, grids, and other mapping tools. They should be able to understand and apply time zones. They need to understand the concept of distance. In addition, they should be able to draw inferences from maps; to compare various maps, to analyze and interpret different kinds of maps, and learn how to create their own maps. Students in enriched social studies courses should be able to read and interpret charts, tables, and other graphics. They also should demonstrate the ability to interpret the meanings of cartoons, photographs, paintings, drawings, and other images relative to social studies topics. The ability to interpret visual images such as pictures and other graphic representations represents is also an important skill of analysis.

Academic vocabulary commonly used in social studies courses

Originally identified by Deborah J. Short (1994), social studies employs four kinds of academic terminology: instructional/directional, concrete, conceptual, and functional. Instructional or directional tools like maps use terms such as north, south, east, west, above, below, etc. Concrete terminology refers to factual information; for example, names of laws like the Stamp Act, of events like the Industrial Revolution, and/or proper names of historical figures; dates or years of historical events, etc. Conceptual vocabulary includes words referring to ideas, such as "democracy," "taxation," "representation," "Enlightenment," "utilitarianism," "supply and demand," etc. Functional vocabulary consists of terms denoting certain academic/cognitive functions or processes, such as "sequencing" events in chronological order. In addition to making sure they know about these kinds of academic vocabularies, teachers should encourage students to use terms from each of these domains during classroom discussions and in their group projects, oral reports, and presentations.

Sequencing and chronology

Gifted students in social studies classes should become familiar with and apply the terminology used for chronology and time elements. Given a series of historical or recent events, they should be able to arrange them in the correct chronological order. They should become familiar with timelines, learn how to read timelines, and develop the ability to create their own timelines. They should learn how to research chronology and time. Gifted students should have or develop an understanding of the concepts of time, change, and continuity. They should have or develop enough facility with sequencing and ordering to enable using these skills to plan and carry out tasks assigned in the social studies class. These organizational skills related to planning and sequencing also benefit them in their other classes in areas such as accomplishing academic tasks and in personal life in areas such as planning and time management.

Bloom's Taxonomy as a reading strategy

Recent research finds a student's academic vocabulary in a subject as most predictive of their success in learning the content of that subject. For literacy in a content area, students must construct meaning from what they read. Using linguistic strategies assists students in finding meaning from interacting with their texts by interpreting, organizing, and retrieving the information they encounter. One way that teachers can help students to do this is by using Bloom's Taxonomy when writing questions for study, discussion, review, and/or testing; and when designing

projects or activities for gifted students. Bloom identifies the following skills, in order of increasing complexity: knowledge, or knowing facts such as names, dates, events, etc.; comprehension, or understanding the facts known; application, or applying understanding to other situations/examples; analysis, or breaking information down into its components; synthesis, or creatively combining/integrating components; and evaluation, or assessing the accuracy, meaning, relevance, utility, and application of information.

Understanding an author's main idea by predicting it

Teachers of enriched social studies to gifted students should realize the various demands that textual material makes of the reader. One such demand is to understand the writer's main idea. Teachers can help students prepare for such understanding by instructing them to anticipate the central concept in the text. Before they begin reading, the teacher can ask students to skim the text first to develop an educated guess regarding the main idea. The teacher should point out to students such clues as the title of the book, chapter, article, or essay; paragraph headings; terms and/or names that are repeated often; etc. The teacher and class should review all of the students' predictions of the key message or concept. They can revisit these predictions after the students have read the text. Then the students can identify which clues they gleaned from skimming the text were useful and which clues were not.

Using vocabulary, associations, and questions

Social studies teachers can help their gifted students prepare for a reading assignment by giving them a chance to preview the academic vocabulary or terminology used in the text. For example, the teacher can use a "word splash," a collection of key terms used in a section of text arrayed on a page with the most central concept or term in the center and related terms around it. The class can discuss these terms for comprehension before reading and for recognition during reading, and the teacher can post them on the wall or board. To make associations or connections, teachers should have students ask themselves what they think they know about the subject before reading. This achieves the dual purposes of uncovering student biases and/or misperceptions, establishing a context for the reading and making them feel familiar with the subject, and stimulating their engagement and interaction with the material.

Critical thinking skills

Gifted students need to develop their skills for analyzing, synthesizing, and evaluating subject content that they read. Students need to realize that anything in print was written by someone. Teachers can help their gifted students discover who wrote or published the essay, article, textbook, eyewitness report, or primary document they are reading. Furthermore, teachers can ask the students to ascertain the author's originally targeted audience, why the author wrote the material, and what purposes the author hoped to accomplish by writing it. Teachers can ask their students to draw inferences about the author's intended audience. Such an activity will help the students learn how to select the best research sources for their own class and independent study projects. Developing their skills in critical reading will help students develop their general critical thinking skills, as well.

Five W's of journalism, comparisons and contrasts, and cause-and-effect relationships

When their social studies students are reading journalistic content such as newspaper or magazine articles, teachers should include in their assignments the identification of the "Five W's" of journalism: Who, What, When, Where, and Why. Answering these questions helps students focus on the key elements of persons, actions, times, places, and reasons in historical or current events. Teachers should call students' attention to comparison/contrast, showing how the author saw similarities and/or differences between/among events, actions, or situations, and why the author found these similarities/differences important. Teachers can show how authors describe cause-and-effect relationships with qualifying phrases like "as one result...", "in part because of...", "this helps to explain...", etc., and then have students compile lists of such qualifiers. Teachers can help students explain authors' causal arguments without agreeing with them and differentiate opinion from fact by asking students how the author explains the causes of an event, rather than asking them what the causes are.

Questions and during-reading strategies

Students learn more from their reading if teachers instruct them to use what they read to answer questions. This focuses their attention on the reading and helps them to apply it. Teachers should encourage advanced readers to think of their own questions and try to answer them through their reading. Many gifted students will already have formed their own questions out of their curiosity about the subject. For gifted students who are younger and/or not as proficient in reading, teachers also can create their own questions and use them as an outline for reading. This will help students to focus their reading to identify key points in the text. Teachers can write these question outlines to focus on the subject content or on student reading and study skills. A teacher also can identify during-reading strategies specific to the textual material to help students self-monitor their comprehension.

Identifying and analyzing writing styles

Gifted students should understand and apply both the content and the writing style in their social studies reading. Teachers can show students various writing approaches in written materials. For example, some authors first will establish the context for a historical event and then recount its details in chronological order of occurrence. Others may open by relating an anecdote and then explain how it illustrates or is related to the topic. Reporters often use a common journalism technique of opening an article with a paragraph summarizing the key points of the report and then filling out these key points in subsequent paragraphs with more details and/or quotations of comments or responses from involved people whom they interviewed or those persons they consulted as expert sources. Teachers can stimulate discussions by asking students to project how each of these styles might influence different reading audiences. They can also provide challenges to gifted students by having them apply the styles in their own writing.

Sequential and causal relationships

Social studies teachers can point out to their gifted students that when authors of reading materials use terms like "...and then...", "next," "subsequently," "thereafter," "later," and "finally" to represent a string of events, this indicates a chronological sequence, but it might or might not also indicate a cause-and-effect relationship. Teachers should advise their students to seek other clues in the writing before they assume that one event or action actually caused the next one. After reading, students still may need support to figure out the author's primary message or argument. Graphic organizers such as concept maps, flow charts, or outlines help students to visualize verbalized ideas. Teachers can have students paraphrase what they read in 3-5 written or spoken sentences to show their comprehension. Paraphrases should include the subject/topic, the main idea, key terms, and the most important details.

Critical thinking relative to importance, chronology, true-false statements, and important issues

After they have read assigned social studies texts, students will benefit if their teachers have them list the most significant points in the material and rank them in order of importance. This will help students clarify priorities among logical points/reasons in an argument, enhancing critical thinking skills. When the time sequence of events is significant, teachers can assign students to list 5-10 chronological events the author has cited. Teachers can help students identify an author's viewpoint by giving them statements to identify as true or false according to the author and having them cite specific pieces of text as the bases for their choices. The teacher also can use true-false statements to help students distinguish authors' opinions from facts. Regarding important issues, teachers can have students evaluate the author's argument, giving sufficient time and teacher guidance. This can motivate further reading and research: in the evaluation process, students will want to consult additional sources.

Exploration of multiple perspectives

Educators advise social studies teachers against adhering to a single source or a narrow definition of sequences of historical or current events. Instead, they recommend encouraging student appreciation of a breadth of perspectives within the subject's topics. Teachers can do this by asking students to consider topics such as: from whose viewpoint an account was written; whether other views or interpretations might exist, and if so, why; whose voices are identified in the account and whose voices are not; what evidence is given in the account for its assertions; how the students can evaluate the quality of that evidence; how specific individuals and/or groups of people are depicted in the account; why they might be depicted in that way; why different accounts of historical events exist; and what influence the existence of varying accounts has on our concepts of historical accuracy and of "truth."

Scavenger hunt

Researchers (Doty, Cameron, and Barton, 2003) indicate that "...teaching reading in social studies is not so much about teaching students basic reading skills as it is about teaching students how to use reading as a tool for thinking and learning." One way teachers can help gifted students construct meaning from text is a "scavenger hunt" through the book. For example: ask them how many chapters and/or sections the book has and how it is organized. Ask what kind of material is at the beginning of the text and the significance of this. Ask them what kinds of skills or techniques the reader may require to read and understand the text. Ask them to identify special features in the student textbook that do not appear in trade books, and how these features can help them to understand and organize the text content. Finally, ask them how their answers to the preceding questions will help them to read the text better, and why.

Differentiated instruction for gifted students in the language arts

Included among differentiation approaches in adapting language arts curricula for gifted students are acceleration; depth, complexity, challenge, and creativity. In differentiating the curriculum for gifted students, teachers must adjust their expectations regarding the demands of content, process, and concept to higher levels. To meet these higher expectation levels, one method is to give students access to more advanced content or curricula when they are younger while still assuring that they can meet prescribed standards at all levels below that. Students also may be allowed to accelerate through the standard curriculum. Either way, teachers must adjust their expectations for advanced student levels. To meet gifted students' needs for advancement, depth, and complexity, one example is: following a class discussion on major themes in novels, a teacher could assign a gifted student to select a novel and write an essay examining how its major themes are treated in one chapter.

Traditionally, instruction in the language arts has placed emphasis on basic reading skills and on assessing those skills by testing lower-level cognitive skills such as factual knowledge rather than fostering active inquiry and learning. Gifted students who have already mastered fundamental reading skills will not be challenged by these traditional methods. Verbally gifted children frequently attain linguistic proficiency at younger ages than their non-gifted age peers. Individual gifted students may be more advanced in a variety of areas in addition to reading, such as literary analysis, writing poetry, and/or writing prose. Gifted students who have mastered basic reading skills are ready before others to apply their abilities to higher-level cognitive tasks such as reading critically, writing exposition, communicating orally with others, developing their vocabularies and language usage, and learning foreign languages. These differences dictate a need for differentiated instruction for verbally gifted students in all developmental stages.

Selecting language arts instructional strategies

According to expert educators, instructional strategies are not differentiated exclusively for students with gifts in the language arts. Rather, the level and character of the particular curriculum being taught is used to determine which instructional strategies are most indicated and how they should be applied. The curriculum and the choice of teaching strategies cannot be separated. Educational researchers and groups such as the National Association for Gifted Children find the diagnostic-prescriptive approach to teaching as of value for the purpose of differentiating language arts instruction for gifted students. This approach affords a process of assessment to determine each individual student's abilities and talents in the language arts, allowing educators to adapt their instruction to meet individual student needs. This lets linguistically gifted students progress at faster paces by not requiring their instruction in skills that they have already mastered.

Effective teaching of gifted students in the language arts

Educational researchers have found that certain instructional strategies can be paired with advanced curricula for effectively teaching gifted students in the language arts. One such strategy is

questioning: when students have read or viewed challenging materials, teachers can stimulate class/group discussions at higher cognitive levels by asking them questions about the material. Another technique teachers can use is to assign open-ended activities. As long as these activities are sufficiently difficult, they can promote learning and growth in gifted students. Another strategy teachers can apply in conjunction with an advanced curriculum found especially effective for gifted students involves giving them poorly structured problems, which facilitates problem-based learning and challenges advanced learners to exercise and develop their problem-solving skills while applying the information and concepts that they have learned at the same time.

Characteristics of good writing programs

For students who display gifts in the language arts, good writing programs should focus on developing the students' skills in expository writing, i.e. informational, descriptive, or explanatory writing; and in persuasive writing, i.e. argumentation, logic, and rhetoric. Teachers need to help gifted students learn the process of writing by concentrating on the components of developing ideas, opinions, and arguments regarding current issues; writing drafts, making revisions, and editing. Educators also should give their gifted students exposure and practice in writing narrative, poetry, and other forms of literature by presenting them with literary models of each form and then assigning them to write their own original work in each form. Students at the high school level can be assigned exercises wherein they copy the styles of their favorite authors. Such an activity helps them to develop control over the medium, develop flexibility and versatility, and eventually develop and identify their own individual writing styles.

Oral communication

To attain a good balance, language arts instruction in the area of oral communication for gifted students should address equally both speaking and listening to oral language. Gifted students should be assisted in developing their skills for evaluative or critical listening— not just hearing, comprehending, and remembering spoken language, but also analyzing, assessing, and judging it for veracity, accuracy, credibility, and relative bias, and distinguishing between facts and opinions. Gifted students should learn and practice the techniques of formal argumentation and debating. In addition, gifted students should practice discussion as another element of oral communication, including asking questions, probing for additional information, and expressing and hearing ideas and then building upon these collaboratively. Students talented in the creative arts will benefit from the opportunity to develop advanced skills in these areas through instruction in oral interpretation and participation in dramatic productions.

Literature

While standard school literature courses afford a number of works of high quality for students to read, gifted students will be expected and will want to go beyond these. High school students can find reading lists of books for pre-college preparation at most public and school libraries. Some gifted students read at such a high level that some of these books may be accessible and suitable for them in middle/junior high or even elementary school. Recommendations from educators include that teachers should emphasize student development of critical reading and thinking skills and help gifted students to develop their skills for analyzing and interpreting the literature. Teachers are also advised that their gifted students should read a broad range of subject matter. They should become familiar with various authors and their contents, themes, and styles. They should also come to recognize which authors are their favorites and learn more about those authors' lives.

Language study

Language study includes the main components of vocabulary grammar, and syntax (i.e. sentence structure and word order). Therefore, instruction in the language arts for gifted students should emphasize the development, extension, and correct use of vocabulary. Instruction should include promoting an understanding of etymology or the origins of words, including word roots, prefixes and suffixes, and their original language sources. Language arts education for gifted students should include making analogies to teach an understanding of relationships between/among concepts and words. Gifted students also should learn linguistics, or the formal study of language; the history of their language; and semantics, or the study of the meanings of words. In teaching language arts to gifted students, the preferred approach integrates all of these elements of language study into one unified program for a holistic appreciation rather than teaching the elements separately on a disconnected piecemeal basis.

Benefits of learning other languages

Verbally gifted students can not only excel in English, but also should learn foreign languages. In fact, foreign language study is one of the areas of curriculum differentiation in language arts instruction for verbally gifted students. Learning other languages enhances understandings of the history and structure of English; exposes students to the histories and cultures of other countries; gives them access to literary, scientific, and other text in foreign languages; and enables proficient students to communicate with persons from other nations and backgrounds. Such instruction even can prepare some students for future diplomatic careers. Learning foreign languages early is advantageous for gifted students. They can and should accelerate through four years of a second language and at least two years of a third. Choosing languages spoken in the community will afford follow-up opportunities. Spanish, French, German, Chinese, and Japanese are good choices. Latin and Greek (also a modern spoken language) are invaluable sources of English word roots.

Visual and performing arts

Persons and groups dedicated to the education of gifted students believe that the visual (drawing, painting, sculpture, photography, cinematography, etc.) and performing (singing, dancing, acting, etc.) arts are essential parts of healthy, productive lives. The Arts Network of the National Association for Gifted Children, for example, finds that "...the health and productivity of a society is reflective of the degree of artistic expression among its citizens." This network thus commits to the initiation, development, and implementation of teaching resources and strategies to support student aptitudes and interests in these areas, including furthering professional and public acknowledgement of the visual and performing arts as a necessary domain of giftedness, promoting more research into the topic of artistic gifts and talents, furnishing practical teaching methods and resources to cultivate artistic expression, and raising educational and public awareness of aesthetic perception, appreciation, values, and expression.

Incorporating arts instruction

Arts instruction reinforces spoken and written communication and gives gifted students more opportunities to use analytical thought and creative problem-solving skills. Having students visually illustrate (draw, paint, etc.) a salient aspect of a story they read and discuss these illustrated aspects in small groups enhances the students' critical thinking skills. Teachers can help students adapt a written story into a dramatic piece, choose the most important scenes, explain their selections, and perform it as actors and narrators. This type of activity stimulates not only analytical thinking, but also imaginative interpretation and reading. Teachers also can have gifted students identify a problem, conflict, or issue in their assigned reading; assign the parts of characters included in the text to different students; and then debate the topic they have identified. This activity can make gifted students more aware of various points of view and of people's different motivations for their behaviors.

Integrating goals and activities in the arts into writing curriculum

To develop gifted students' skills for synthesizing information, teachers can have them use a variety of sources such as paintings, photographs, musical compositions, and literature or other written work, to write an essay, script, poem, or sketch about some current event they find reported in a newspaper. The teacher can assign students to write an account of this event from various points of view, such as their best friend; their mother; their father; their sister; their brother; their family's pet dog, cat, or other animal; their teacher; etc. This helps students explore both the variety of sources for news stories and the variety of perspectives afforded by different individuals, as well as helping them to synthesize disparate elements. Another

Copyright © Mometrix Media. You have been licensed one copy of this document for personal use only. Any other reproduction or redistribution is strictly prohibited. All rights reserved.

writing exercise integrating the arts involves having students listen to and analyze a musical composition and then write a script for a conversation analogous to the music in tone, tempo (speed/pace), divisions, and changes in speed, pitch, etc.

Teachers can use paintings, photos, and other visual art as catalysts to stimulate their gifted students to generate novel story ideas to write. They can suggest that the students use the visuals to correspond with their story's climax, its rising action just before the climax, or its dénouement (falling action). Teachers can give gifted students practice doing investigative research by first giving them a story to read about a painting that vanished, and then having them imagine and write about how they, as "art detectives," recovered it. Teachers can assign students to write fictional pieces about uncovering art forgeries, including the telltale details. To give them experience with understanding various perspectives, teachers can have gifted students write historical fiction about the origins of famous artworks and points along their journeys to their eventual/current destinations. They can write from the viewpoint of the artist, people in possession of the art, people searching for it, or the artwork itself.

Learning in the arts to the cognitive and academic development

Educational research has found that in addition to developing gifted students' creative abilities, instruction in the arts also enhances their cognitive and academic accomplishments. Art education improves the student's observational skills, abstract thinking skills, analytical skills, and problem-solving skills. In creating works of art, artists must use their reasoning powers to identify and define problems, to visualize and establish their goals, select methods for gathering information, propose solutions to problems, evaluate their solutions, and use their imaginations to revise those solutions. Therefore, the creative process in the arts requires, develops, and exercises higher-level cognitive skills. Teachers can integrate the arts into their curriculum and design activities tailored to gifted students' unique abilities, needs, and interests, and challenge them with increasing sophistication and complexity in the activities. Educational researchers advise teachers designing parallel curricula or differentiated instruction to clarify their students' educational goals before developing alternative instruction. Arts learning goals and activities can be integrated into math, science, language arts, and social studies curricula.

Value of integrating the arts with academic subjects

Academically successful gifted students will have gained much experience with using their superior skills of reasoning, abstract thinking, and problem solving in academic subjects such as mathematics, sciences, language arts, and social studies. But when the arts are integrated into these subjects, and reciprocally, elements of academic subjects are integrated into artistic activities, gifted students can apply these advanced cognitive skills in different ways that may be new to them. This type of activity promotes cognitive flexibility and supports the gifted student's diversity of interests. These novel applications of their skills are also facilitated when students experience what Csikszentmihalyi called "flow," the immersion in the creative process wherein time seems to stop, the artist becomes one with the art, and creation is spontaneous and effortless. With curricular integration of arts and academics, gifted students can contribute more of their unique abilities, insights, and visions, and make original discoveries and innovations.

Integrating arts goals and activities into social studies curriculum

Teachers can help their gifted students to associate the arts with social studies and vice versa by helping students relate such things as art movements with their social and historical contexts and events. For example, a teacher can ask gifted students to imagine they are time-traveling news journalists who visit the past to report on artistic movements such as Cubism or Expressionism. The teacher can assign the students to write newspaper articles telling how the historical, political, intellectual/philosophical, and social milieu and circumstances of the period influenced a movement in art. Students also can write about how the art movement influenced the thinking of the period in turn. They can explain how the art movement reflected the times and changes occurring, how the movement demonstrated a break from previous traditions, and how this break reflected and influenced historical and social developments.

Integrating learning in the arts into math and science curricula

Although people sometimes consider math and science as dealing with facts and objective reality rather than the arts because artists may represent and manipulate reality according to their own perceptions and the messages they want to impart, the arts and sciences actually are closely related. For example, the musical compositions of J.S. Bach follow mathematical formulae and their structures can be analyzed mathematically. Perspective and color are sciences used in drawing and painting, as are anatomy and physiology used in portraiture. Famous Renaissance polymath Leonardo da Vinci not only did work far ahead of his time in both the arts and the sciences, he also integrated these fields in everything he produced.

Contemporary artist Thomas Locker has created portfolio formats specially designed for teachers to use in classrooms. They combine his beautiful paintings of nature subjects with information and activities that teachers can use to foster scientific inquiry by gifted students.

Giving an example involving perception, physical reality, and illusion

In both the arts and the sciences, we encounter illusions wherein things are not really as they seem. Optical and auditory illusions can be created and explained in the sciences, and artists often deliberately create illusions to communicate a specific idea with their respective audiences. Teachers can expose their gifted students to various styles of visual art such as Impressionist, Surrealist, and trompe l'oeil techniques; to experimental art; to performance art such as modern dance performances; and other presentations. They can have students write down their observational analyses of the artists' assumptions about the nature of physical matter, e.g. whether matter is static or in perpetual motion; whether it is solid or not; its weight, speed, etc. Students then can use the laws and principles of physics to examine these assumptions. Finally, teachers can assign students to write essays challenging or defending the artistic renderings.

Integrating the arts into science curriculum

Teachers can give their gifted students exercises in applying particular scientific principles or concepts to solving problems in creating art. For example, they can assign students to explore the scientific subject of light. The teacher can assemble a group of paintings notable in their treatments of light (e.g. Rembrandt,

Monet, Turner, and others) and ask students to discuss the manner in which each artist depicts light's interaction with color and with water, the directions of light in the paintings, the quality of indoor and outdoor light, the quality of outdoor light at different times of day, how this affects colors, etc. The teacher also can ask gifted students to choose some aspect of light of scientific interest to them and then to participate as artists themselves by coming up with ways in which they can express this aspect of light visually via sketches, drawings, paintings, collages, sculptures, etc.

Enhancing the ability of visual perception and the ability to estimate mathematical quantities

When creating visual, especially representational art, artists frequently self-assess their visual perceptions against reality by estimating objective distances, sizes, heights, widths, and areas in the physical world. Teachers can provide their gifted students with comparable experiences through real-world experiments. For example, they can go outside on a sunny day in an area with some trees, each push a stick into the ground, measure the length that is above ground, and then measure the length of the stick's shadow. Then they can measure the length of a nearby tree's shadow. The teacher then asks them how they can calculate the height of the tree, in inches and in feet, based on the information they have. Teachers should allow gifted students to come up with their own methods for solving the problem, including drawing diagrams, taking photographs, or whatever they want to try. This activity sharpens accuracy in both visual perception and numerical estimation.

Development wherein further research is needed according to experts in the field

Educational researchers specializing in gifted education find that many aspects of the social and emotional development of gifted individuals have not been researched nearly as much as the intellectual and academic aspects of their development. They recommend that researchers, school psychologists, guidance counselors, and other professionals can contribute to exploration of the affective domain. Asynchronous development in cognitive vs. affective domains has long been observed in the gifted, but it demands further study, as does perfectionism in the gifted. Scientists also want more research into underachievement, depression, eating disorders, self-injurious behaviors, and substance abuse relative to giftedness, as well as responses to life events such as divorce, loss and grief, serious illness, injury, and relocating. Additionally, research into giftedness is lacking related to obsessive-compulsive disorder, sexual abuse, physical disabilities, Asperger's syndrome, serious conflicts between parents and their gifted children, and problematic developmental transitions.

Supporting the development of gifted students

Gifted education programs, both inside and outside of general education classrooms, should incorporate curriculum elements designed to support emotional, social, and career development in gifted students. At all age/grade levels, school curricula can be proactive by including psychoeducational knowledge regarding the way in which giftedness influences these developmental domains. When teaching social sciences and literature, teachers can give assignments related to the psychosocial aspects of these subjects. Classes can have group discussions about developmental challenges. Career and talent development often present issues for gifted children at much younger ages than for other students, so these topics should be addressed in the curriculum. Viewing and addressing underachievement and high achievement from a developmental perspective can help both students and educators. Teachers should affirm student resiliency and personal strengths, which can be eclipsed by performance/underperformance. Advocates for legislation, funding, and services for gifted students also should emphasize affective considerations in their efforts.

How common characteristics of gifted children can influence their affective development

The developmental tasks for gifted children are the same as for all children. For example, all children must develop such concepts as a sense of identity, a sense of self-efficacy, differentiation of self, relationships with peers, autonomy in life and in school, and paths toward careers. But gifted children can experience these developmental milestones quite differently from other children. Researchers find gifted children are commonly more emotionally sensitive, intense, and overly excitable. They also are commonly more perceptive about human behaviors and personalities; along with their talents, their moral development is precocious, so they tend to have different concerns at higher cognitive levels and younger ages than other children. Even the faster cognitive processing of gifted youngsters can intensify their emotional responses to external stimuli. These common gifted characteristics may sometimes impede developmental processes. Therefore educators, parents, counselors, psychologists, and psychiatrists working

with gifted students should possess adequate and accurate knowledge regarding these children's affective development.

Individual differences within the population of gifted students

Social contexts such as geographic residence, socioeconomic status, and cultural background affect personal, family, and community definitions of giftedness. Some groups place high value on academic success. Other groups place higher value on creativity, while yet other groups place higher value on adaptability, i.e. ability to adjust to changing circumstances, including fitting into a social group, more than excellence. Finally, some cultures place priority on the value of service to others. Multiple types of giftedness exist besides intellectual ability. Even within that one type, emotional and social factors are significant considerations. The range of measured IQs among gifted students is as large as the range in general education classrooms. Differences between a moderately gifted child and an extremely gifted child can mirror differences between a child of low-average ability and a moderately gifted child. Psychologically and socially, variation is as great among gifted students as between gifted students and others. Increased variation can increase social problems. Nonetheless, because all gifted students vary in social adjustment, educators are also cautioned against making assumptions about social issues.

Mental health considerations

Research finds gifted students no more prone to experience mental health problems than are other students. Nonetheless, if educators and counselors have limited knowledge and experience of gifted students, their perceptions can be influenced by exclusively positive stereotypes of the gifted. Such a perception can be dangerous, in that adults may not recognize, and hence not address, counseling needs and/or developmental issues in gifted students. Some gifted characteristics can become liabilities in this sense. Also, adults unfamiliar with gifted students' specific characteristics may incorrectly interpret some divergent behaviors as pathological symptoms. Another consideration is that gifted students, wanting to preserve their competent reputations and avoid disappointing invested adults, often do not request needed assistance. Adults who are both uninformed regarding the complexity of gifted students' concerns and also dazzled by the gifted students' abilities are less objective, can overlook students' vulnerabilities, and cannot work effectively with them. Adult respect for gifted students is more appropriate than awe. As in curriculum and instruction, differentiation in counseling services is indicated for the gifted.

Attitude of experts toward the affective development of gifted students

As many experts in gifted education assert, gifted students deserve for adults to attend not only to their gifts, talents, and performance, but also to their overall wellbeing. Gifted children go through developmental processes and achievements universal to all children, although they may experience these processes and achievements differently. They also have other developmental experiences unique to each individual. Because educators and other adults so frequently focus on the academic and creative potential of gifted students and their performance or lack thereof, they may not focus enough on the affective dimension of their development. Adults need to remember that gifted students' developmental progress is not only cognitive, but also emotional, social, and

career-related. Moreover, progress in cognitive and academic areas also has emotional and social effects. Thus, organizations such as the National Association for Gifted Children take the position that teachers, administrators, and counselors in schools should deliberately, proactively nurture the emotional and social development of gifted students.

Under-representation in gifted education programs

Experts in the field of gifted education have emphasized the necessity of using multiple assessment instruments and criteria for determining student gifts requiring special educational programming. However, too often the need for additional assessments is determined by an initial standardized test score. Such tests can overlook many gifted students. Factors interfering with student performance on standardized tests and/or in the classroom include: difficult life circumstances, lack of parental support, minority cultural values and behaviors, lack of language proficiency, disabilities, depression, lack of faith or trust in schools, behavioral issues, and illness. When such factors prevent identification, gifted students lose opportunities to have their abilities acknowledged and cultivated and opportunities for social access with their intellectual peers. Even identified gifted students frequently have to adjust themselves to a program, instead of the program's adjustment to accommodate students' abilities, as should occur. Without individualization, "one-size-fits-all" programs can cause frustration and discomfort to immigrant, minority, low-income, and underachieving gifted students.

Student gifts and talents as assets

While superior intellectual abilities and/or creative talents may seem obvious assets, a number of factors have contributed to this view's overshadowing the recognition of less beneficial aspects of giftedness. Accordingly, samples selected for quantitative research studies have not covered a wide enough range of the gifted population. By not including sufficient socioeconomic, cultural, and performance factors in sampling, studies do not reflect the true range of issues for gifted students. In addition, such research findings inform the development of instruments for assessment and intervention, which in turn will not adequately represent "non-asset" aspects of giftedness. Also, due to the paucity of qualitative studies on gifted students, researchers are limited in understanding feelings and thoughts that gifted students have not expressed to others. Other factors include our society's emphasis on equality, and legislation mandating educational accountability and achievement, both of which are not conducive to addressing gifted students' emotional and social needs.

Problem solving as a team

If a group of gifted students wants to solve a problem as a team, the first stage they should address involves understanding the nature of the specific problem. That accomplished, in the second stage they would brainstorm ideas for potential solutions to the problem. Once they had a number of possible solutions, the third stage would involve deciding what to do. Dr. E. Paul Torrance, who developed the most widely used standardized tests of creative thinking, founded the Future Problem Solving Program (FPSP) in 1974. Today it is used with hundreds of thousands of students, nationwide and in several other countries. The FPSP model contains three

sections and six steps: Under the first section, Understanding the Problem, steps 1 and 2 are identifying challenges in the problem, and selecting an underlying problem. The second section, Generating Ideas, has step 3, producing solution ideas. The third section, Planning for Action, includes steps 4, 5, and 6: generating and selecting criteria, applying criteria, and developing an action plan.

Services to gifted students from minority groups

It has long been a concern of educators that gifted children with lower socioeconomic levels and those children with some minority cultures and/or languages have not been represented sufficiently in gifted educational programs. Such students also often have gifts not as easily evaluated by traditional measurement instruments. Thus, these students have not been afforded opportunities to develop and apply their gifts fully. In 1988, the National Educational Longitudinal Study found a significant level of under-service by gifted and talented programs to students from economically disadvantaged backgrounds. This study also found varying levels of service to different student minority groups. The National Academy of Sciences reported in 2003 that minority students were overrepresented in special education and underrepresented in gifted education. The National Research Council reported that 9.9% of Asian students and 7.47% of white students in America were placed in gifted programs, while only 4.86% of Native American, 3.57% of Hispanic, and 3.04% of African-American students were identified as gifted.

Counselor preparation specifically for working with gifted students

Giftedness has significant impacts on the emotional and social development of

- 70 -

young people. They encounter the same universal developmental transitions and challenges as all children, yet they are likely to experience them quite differently. In addition, they experience other, individualized developmental issues. They will be concerned with moral, academic, and career issues at younger ages than other students. They may also have concerns that other students do not experience at any age. The issues that concern these gifted students have ramifications for their overall wellbeing. Thus school counselors and outside, private counselors must possess knowledge regarding the characteristics of gifted students. Knowing about the emotional intensity and hypersensitivity of many gifted students keeps counselors from misinterpreting these as abnormal. Knowledge of gifted students' characteristics can explain classroom and/or social problems and afford more perspective on developmental issues. This knowledge also should inform counselors' case studies and intervention plans.

Creative problem-solving

Participating in creative problem-solving develops the higher-order cognitive skills of gifted students, which helps them to apply their knowledge for solving problems. According to experts, there is more emphasis in this process on learning "how to think" than on acquiring information. Creative problem-solving helps gifted students enhance their analytical skills as well as their creative abilities. It builds their skills in spoken and written communication and encourages gifted students to develop skills for conducting research and improving these skills. When gifted students participate in groups to solve problems creatively as a team, the process contributes to their developing responsibility as group members. The creative problem-solving process provides gifted students with guidance that enables them to develop not only responsibility, but also more self-direction. This process also furnishes gifted students with a model for problem-solving they can incorporate into their lives. Moreover, it engages gifted students' interest in the future.

Underachievement in gifted students from minority backgrounds

Low self-esteem in general hampers student achievement. Researchers also find that poor self-concepts specific to academics and social interactions interfere. Some researchers have emphasized the need to consider the strength and/or positivity of a gifted minority student's sense of racial/ethnic identity. Students whose racial identities are not positive can be more susceptible to counterproductive peer pressure. They also may associate academic achievement with the dominant culture, hence with betraying their minority culture, i.e. "selling out" or trying to "act white." This view results in less effort, which results in less achievement. Psychologically, with a high internal locus of control, a student attributes his or her achievement to ability and effort and is more likely to achieve. Minority students who expect external factors such as discrimination and injustice to block their success demonstrate a high external locus of control and are less likely to achieve up to their potentials.

Researchers have found that among gifted black students, for example, underachieving students have reported experiencing less positive teacher-student interactions, less supportive classroom climates, insufficient time to understand lesson material, and feeling uninterested and unmotivated toward school. They also attributed part of their lack of interest to their schools' lack of multicultural education. Teachers often have lowered expectations of minority and low-income students, especially for teachers with inadequate preparation in both gifted education and multicultural education. Such teachers are less likely to refer minority students for gifted education services, and with lower expectations they are also less likely to identify these students as underachievers. Without access to suitable educational services that address their individual strengths and needs, minority gifted students can become frustrated, bored, lose interest in school, and become underachievers.

Mismatches between learning styles and teaching styles

The predominant cultural values in America favor individualism, competition, and excellence in individual achievement, both in society and in school. In contrast, many other countries have cultures that value collectivism, cooperation, and placing the good of the group ahead of one's individual concerns. Therefore, many students belonging to minority groups in the United States have cultural values that more closely reflect the values of other countries of origin than the majority American values. These students tend to be more social and cooperative in their attitudes and behaviors, and less individualistic and competitive. Teaching styles in America tend to place emphasis on competing with others to be the best. Too much emphasis on competition can interfere with minority gifted students' achievement: rather than increasing their motivation, competition can decrease motivation by provoking anxiety and by negatively influencing students' social and academic self-images.

The majority of teaching methods in public schools tend to use the verbal modality, to deal in abstract concepts, and to teach concepts and skills in isolation, i.e. taken out of context. These methods contrast markedly with the learning styles of many minority students. For example, research finds that black students are more likely to be visual rather than verbal learners, i.e. they learn better using visual images than words. In addition, black students are more likely to be field-dependent rather than field-independent learners, meaning that they rely on the surrounding context to understand the material presented and will not grasp it as well (or at all) when it is presented out of context. Finally, the research indicates that black students tend to learn more concretely rather than abstractly, so teaching abstract concepts through using concrete objects rather than presenting such concepts only in abstract terms would enhance their learning. Mismatched teaching methods produce confusion and frustration in students with these learning styles, thereby leading to underachievement.

Supportive strategies educators can use

Educators should give minority gifted students opportunities to talk about their concerns with teachers and counselors. In addition, educators should employ more collaborative and cooperative group learning methods, as well as verbal and other positive reinforcements. They should reduce norm-referenced and competitive contexts, set high expectations for minority gifted students, and teach for mastery. They should try different teaching modalities such as concrete/abstract, visual/auditory, etc. to identify students' learning styles, strengths, and needs. They should accommodate their instruction to student learning styles. Educators should attend to issues students may have with self-perceptions, self-efficacy (self-perceived ability to accomplish tasks), and motivation. Classrooms should be student-centered and address affective needs. Teaching and counseling techniques should be multicultural. Educators also should enlist significant involvement by students' parents and other family members and engage role models and mentors for their minority gifted students.

Strategies to help minority gifted students develop internal motivation, self-efficacy, and academic motivation

For intrinsic motivation and self-efficacy, educators should give minority gifted students consistent and constructive feedback, concentrate on individual students' interests, and provide them with choices. In addition, they should alternate their teaching styles to accommodate different student learning styles and furnish projects, simulations, internships, case studies, role plays, and other activities that promote experiential, active, hands-on learning. Educators can provide mentors and role models for students, as well as relevant, inspirational biographies. They can also use bibliotherapy. Teachers should work to establish classrooms with affirming and nurturing atmospheres for minority gifted students and all other students, as well. Teachers should use multicultural instruction that is meaningful personally, relevant culturally, and promotes self-understanding and insights. Some remedial strategies to improve student performance in specific deficit areas include counseling, tutoring, teaching study skills, test-taking skills, organizational and time-management skills, assigning journaling, making learning contracts, and teaching individually and to small groups.

Affective process models

The affective domain relates to the emotions, emotional responses to the environment, and interactions with the social environment, including an individual's motivation, attitudes, perceptions, and values. Some process models used in gifted education focus on this domain. Krathwohl's Taxonomy of the Affective Domain is one such model. It contains five levels: (1) Receiving: Students show awareness of and attention to stimuli presented by teachers. (2) Responding: Students commit to discovery, seek out learning activities, and feel satisfaction from participating in the process. (3) Valuing: Students demonstrate decision-making about a value, their engagement with it, and their commitment to it. At this level, students may endeavor to convince others to commit to a value they have chosen. (4) Organizing: Students construct a belief system/value system, including attitudes, which they organize by the interrelationships of its components. (5) Characterizing by a value or set: Students have organized and internalized their value system and can apply it to many circumstances as a philosophy of life.

Virtual learning environment (VLE)

A virtual learning environment is a computer-based environment where learning materials can be delivered to students via the Internet. By computer information technology, teachers can differentiate their instruction for gifted and talented students. Enhancing school projects by using online databases, scanning images, and incorporating hyperlinks and video clips into them is generally more motivating to students with all levels of ability. VLEs are useful for developing cultural experiences in the visual, performing, and/or creative arts. Students can visit museums, art galleries, government agencies, various industries, and institutions using VLEs. Teachers can acquaint students with a variety of ideas through online exposure to famous and/or controversial individuals. In subjects incorporating research activities, VLEs can give opportunities to gifted students for more advanced learning. Because of the virtually limitless amounts of information accessible on the World-Wide Web and the way it is instantaneously transmitted, using VLEs is a method that students find motivational and exciting.

Cognitive process models

Educational scientists develop theoretical models and then apply the models to instructional approaches and methods. Some models focus on a particular domain, such as affective or cognitive. Cognitive process models focus on the cognitive domain, i.e. mental processes by which students learn and think. Bloom's Taxonomy, created by Benjamin Bloom in 1956, remains one of the most famous and popularly used cognitive process models. This taxonomy contains six ascending levels of cognitive processes: (1) Knowledge: Students can recall (retrieve from memory) or recognize (identify upon presentation) specific information they have learned. (2) Comprehension: Students not only remember, but understand, information they learn. (3) Application: Students can learn ideas, principles, and theories and then apply them to other contexts. (4) Analysis: Students can break information down into component parts. (5) Synthesis: Students can take constituent parts and think originally and creatively to combine them into a whole. (6) Evaluation: Students develop standards and criteria and apply these to concepts, methods, and materials presented to judge their value.

Challenges

An ever-increasing challenge in our schools is that due to economic considerations, school budgets are being cut, and special or supplementary services to gifted students often are eliminated. As a result, general education teachers find they have more gifted and talented students in their classrooms. Their challenge involves meeting the educational needs of students with average ability, students with high ability, students with disabilities whose inclusion in regular classrooms is mandated by law, and students with both gifts and disabilities. Teaching the same curriculum to all students, i.e. teacher-centered instruction, is no longer feasible. Information technology recently has become popular for use with gifted students. As such, information technology can replace some existing delivery methods and be added to others to enhance them. Assistive technology also aids students with vision, hearing, physical, and other disabilities. Those students with both gifts and disabilities receive multiple benefits from technology. Students can work at their own paces, access multiple modalities, select preferred modalities, and learn in more depth through enriched learning experiences.

Thematic units

Teachers use thematic units as a way of incorporating complex, abstract concepts into the curriculum. Thematic units are organized around a particular theme or topic. This organization provides a focus for learning abstract ideas and appeals to areas of student interest. One way that a teacher can employ both thematic units and information technology is to select the content for an integrated thematic unit and then develop a virtual learning environment (VLE) for teaching it. Today there are many Internet websites containing teacher resources, including those for thematic units. For example, the site A-Z Teacher Stuff offers thematic units on topics such as magnets, oceans, Martin Luther King Jr., Harry Potter, and many other themes, including lesson plans for teachers, class activities, etc. The website of the C.O.O.R. Intermediate

School District in Michigan provides additional examples of integrated thematic units.

Websites that teachers can use

Once teachers have selected the content for a lesson or unit they want to deliver in a virtual (computer) environment, they can take advantage of such websites as The Educator's Reference Desk, where they can find lesson plans for any grade level or school subject. In addition to getting help creating and delivering lesson plans, teachers can incorporate hyperlinks from these sites in the virtual learning environments they create for students. Students can follow these links to access virtual lessons providing content enriching the teacher's basic lesson or unit. In addition to lesson plans, teachers can find online student projects and activities, instructional materials, and virtual "field" trips. In virtual trips, students can visit otherwise inaccessible nations, museums, galleries, institutions, organizations, and corporations all over the world. Education World, Eduscapes' Digital and Virtual Museums, and the Museum of Science and Industry are examples of websites offering virtual museum tours.

Intrinsic Motivation Principle of Creativity

While what Renzulli has termed "schoolhouse giftedness" is more easily identified via IQ test scores and more amenable to academic success than what he called "creative-productive giftedness, " which is not as easily identified via IQ test scores. Social psychologists conducting research into creative production over 25 years have found it associated with students' motivational orientations, and those orientations are influenced by environmental factors. They find that internal motivation encourages creativity, while external motivation discourages creativity—this finding is called the Intrinsic Motivation Principle of Creativity. Intrinsically motivated students do tasks for their own sake because they enjoy them, so their rewards come from within them. In contrast, extrinsically motivated students do tasks for a reward coming from outside them.

Characteristics of gifted students relative to achievement motivation

Researchers have discovered that when gifted students consistently bring high skill levels to schoolwork, externally imposed limitations that represent threats to their senses of self-determination are particularly likely to affect them negatively. Gifted children frequently know they have the ability to exceed their non-gifted peers in performance; therefore, they do not rely as much on external rewards, the contingencies for earning them, or feedback from teachers. A more important need for them involves preserving their internal motivation, which cannot be forced or learned, but can too easily be quashed. While research finds gifted students as typically highly motivated, it also finds that motivation in classrooms is problematic for them. This finding is attributable to gifted students not responding well to rigidly structured, specific tasks or assignments, which non-gifted students often need. Since gifted students are self-motivated instead of teacher-motivated, gifted students perform better when given choices, flexibility, and unstructured tasks.

Environmental constraints that stifle creativity

Researchers (e.g. Amabile, 1983a, 1996; Hennessey, 1996) have identified five environmental constraints that destroy internal motivation and creativity:

(1) Expected Reward – students work to receive some externally bestowed reinforcement, rather than being internally motivated to be creative for its enjoyment.
(2) Expected Evaluation – students limit creative exploration, working instead to score well on a test.
(3) Competition – rather than exploring a subject creatively to see where it leads, students focus on besting other students by obtaining the highest scores. Such competition limits creativity, since students' pursuits are narrowed to traditional academic tasks and to achieving the best among typical student responses rather than anything original or different.
(4) Surveillance – when students know they are being observed, they feel less free to engage in creative exploration or find divergent solutions. They are more likely to conform and less likely to be creative.
(5) Time Limits – when students know they are being timed, they feel pressured. Finishing on time interferes with the additional learning and production afforded by creativity.

Environmental influences that affect motivation

Although one might expect gifted students' exceptional abilities to support them in their classroom performance, research finds that gifted students are also very sensitive to influences they encounter in the classroom environment. While enthusiasm for learning and for subject content is a common characteristic of gifted children, teachers can dampen this enthusiasm when they insist that students conform to traditional classroom procedures and behaviors.

Because gifted children often think and do things differently, trying to make them conform can ruin their motivation. They lose interest and get bored. In addition, many gifted children, especially younger ones, frequently do not know how to handle adults' high expectations, how to conduct successful interpersonal interactions, or how to set suitable goals for themselves. All of these factors in combination can contribute to academic underachievement. Underachievement actually is one of the most frequent problems among gifted students.

Fostering creative performance

Educational researchers find that modifying curriculum, using alternative materials, encouraging brainstorming, and teaching strategies for thinking "outside the box" are all necessary, these strategies alone are not sufficient. Teachers, students, parents, and administrators need to collaborate to affect changes in the entire climate of our schools at every level, as well as in the environments of individual classrooms. Some gifted education programs developed in recent decades can be individualized to meet the needs and interests of each specific student. Instead of identifying only students who excel in traditional school subjects, programs taking this alternate approach acknowledge student talents and strengths across a broader range of dimensions. Researchers find the motivation of gifted/talented students is especially susceptible to classroom environmental influences, even more so among the culturally diverse and/or economically deprived. Experts call for educational reform that does not require money so much as commitment to change and willingness to collaborate to make school environments nurture internal motivation and creativity.

Selecting curriculum materials

Gifted students need greater breadth and depth of knowledge and processes than are afforded by school textbooks. When selecting curriculum materials for gifted students, teachers should consider the following curriculum design features:

(1) The purpose and rationale of the curriculum design should be clear.
(2) Selected materials should address objectives for each lesson.
(3) Materials should include appropriate, stimulating, and challenging activities for gifted students.
(4) Materials should include instructional strategies suitable for gifted students that teachers can use.
(5) The materials should include valid and reliable assessment procedures teachers can use to assess the effectiveness of instruction using those materials.
(6) References for additional materials and resources should be provided.
(7) Ideas for extension of the curriculum, activities, and materials should be given.
(8) Technology should be incorporated in the materials. Today many materials are available on websites, which are most likely to adhere to the preceding guidelines.

When teaching gifted students, teachers will find that while these students often master textbook content easily, they also demand broader and more in-depth knowledge of a subject than textbooks afford. As they seek additional curriculum materials for gifted students, teachers should consider their special needs. Specifically, students with higher levels of ability need to be presented with more sophisticated ideas than others and more challenging activities than those usually offered in general education classrooms. Choosing activities that can be individually tailored to any specific student will give teachers more options for optimally meeting individual gifted students' educational requirements. Curriculum materials chosen for gifted students should require more use of higher-order cognitive skills than for other students. Teachers should select materials that incorporate relevant major themes, contain high levels of abstraction, allow student exploration according to their interests, and enable them to create products.

Protecting intrinsic motivation and creative performance

Social psychologists and other educational researchers have amassed a body of literature over 30 years regarding intrinsic motivation, creative performance, and how to promote these attributes in the classroom. Research increasingly has produced evidence that educational reforms to make our schools more conducive to internal motivation and creativity can benefit all students, not merely gifted students. Some steps that have been suggested (Hennessey, 2005) to accomplish such reforms include the following: Teachers need to make every effort to create atmospheres in their classrooms wherein students feel in control of their learning processes. Teachers and school administrators need to attain some distance and perspective in order to make objective, critical reviews of their schools' current reward systems and the types of incentives used. In addition, when external rewards are being used, educators need to help students achieve distance from the limitations these impose. Educators must help students develop proficiency in knowing their own weaknesses and strengths.

Content and process

As Renzulli (2000) defines them, content equals authentic knowledge and process equals teaching techniques. Within the area of content, when selecting curriculum materials, teachers should consider: the organization of the content, the depth in which the content covers its subject, the accuracy of the content, and the degree to which the content moves from concrete topics to abstract concepts. Within the area of process, teachers should consider: opportunities to use/learn problem-solving skills, opportunities to use/develop communication skills, activities that exercise skills of reasoning, relevant connections among parts of the subject area, providing multiple representations of concepts to be taught, opportunities for students to verify their speculations when indicated, opportunities for students to work both individually and in groups, and opportunities for students to use divergent thinking in responding to a lesson, exercise, or activity.,

Difficulties in writing curricula

Curriculum writing can be quite difficult and time-consuming. Difficulties include trying to comply with state curriculum guidelines, feeling pressured to include activities currently popular in the educational community, trying to achieve a balance between content (information/knowledge) and process (teaching/learning), and juggling all these demands. Moreover, the results of these efforts often do not further education or impart meaning to it. Seeking to improve curriculum writing and believing that teachers need time and tools to create meaningful teaching units based on desired outcomes named in a curriculum guide, Renzulli et al (2000) of the University of Connecticut's National Research Center on the Gifted and Talented produced the Multiple Menu

Model of curriculum development. Differentiating this model from more traditional approaches are its stronger emphases on encouraging original inquiry by students, on examining the organization and interrelatedness of knowledge, and on arriving at a balance between content and process.

Multiple Menu Model of curriculum development

While its authors originally conceived of the Multiple Menu Model of curriculum development as a means for differentiating instruction to address the needs of gifted and talented students, Renzulli remarks that teachers can also use it to promote original inquiry and creativity in students at all levels. This model uses the term "menu" to indicate that teachers are able to choose from among many options within each menu. The six component menus are: the Knowledge Menu, addressing the specific subject areas; the Instructional Objectives and Student Activities Menu, Instructional Strategies Menu, Instructional Sequences Menu, and Artistic Modification Menu, all of which address various aspects of pedagogy, i.e. instructional techniques; and the Instructional Products Menu, consisting of the interrelated Concrete Products and Abstract Products Menus, which address the kinds of products the student may create based on the knowledge acquired, and how students as primary inquirers construct this knowledge.

Components of curriculum writing

In curriculum writing, the stated instructional objectives and the specified student activities are concerned with the processes students use in constructing knowledge (for example, analysis, synthesis, and application). These processes are both cognitive and affective in nature. When curriculum writers include both variety and balance among these processes in the activities they design, they enable gifted students to practice using a fuller range of the encoding, decoding, and recoding processes involved in learning new ideas, principles, and information. Instructional strategies represent another area wherein curriculum writers should provide variety. Teachers can use class discussions, student dramatizations of topics, and independent study projects, for example, affording gifted students different ways to learn and utilizing broader ranges of abilities and learning styles. The Multiple Menu Model of curriculum development's Instructional Sequences Menu is a rubric teachers can use with any teaching technique/strategy to help them present lessons in the most effective order.

Selection of representative topics for a curriculum

In developing curricula, teachers must select topics that illustrate a subject's fundamental principles and characteristic concepts. Both traditional models of curriculum development and more progressive ones, such as the National Research Center on the Gifted and Talented's Multiple Menu Model of curriculum development (Renzulli et al, 2000) take into account the students' ages, maturity levels, prior knowledge, and levels of experience. These methods differ in that traditional instructional models typically require teachers to cover a whole textbook with their classes by the end of the term or year; however, the Multiple Menu Model asks teachers instead to narrow down, from all potential texts, chapters, or other sources of information, those few that best represent the concepts and principles of the subject area. This model's authors recommend using a three-phase approach to choosing content: intensive group coverage, extensive group coverage, and intensive individual or small group coverage.

Procedural safeguards related to the educational placement of gifted students

While the federal government has mandated procedural safeguards for the educational placement of students with disabilities, federal laws do not specifically address the placement of students who are gifted without disabilities. Each state Department of Education issues its own set of procedural safeguards for the placement of gifted students. They typically derive these standards from the federal requirements for students with disabilities in that all students must receive a free, appropriate public education (FAPE). Some common safeguards across states include the following standards: districts must give parents prior notice of initiation or refusal to identify, evaluate, place, or provide a FAPE to a gifted student, in the parents' primary communicative mode. Parents must be given copies of procedural safeguards. Written informed parent consent is required before providing individual formal evaluation or initial service to a gifted student, and such consent is voluntary and revocable before the action. Parents have the right to view their child's educational records and participate in educational planning meetings.

Judging the quality of a gifted program or school

Parents should be able to identify the philosophy and goals of a gifted program and/or school. Because giftedness is a lifelong trait, gifted students' academic needs will have some continuity. If program goals differ by age, these differences should reflect instructional variation, which should be both age-appropriate and appropriate for gifted students. Gifted programs should include both acceleration, i.e. offering instruction at a faster pace more suitable for gifted students; and enrichment, i.e. extending the curriculum by increasing the depth of study of a subject appropriately to gifted students' abilities and needs. Another essential factor involves offering multiple options in gifted education. Students gifted in the language arts are different from those gifted in math; mildly gifted and profoundly gifted students differ from one another. Owing to individual differences such as personalities and learning styles, even students with similar levels of giftedness in the same subjects can be very different. As a result, it is critical to include multiple ways to address these multiple educational needs.

Many times, schools depend on a teacher's recommendation or results of a single standardized group test to identify a student for gifted placement. Such methods typically overlook gifted students who are underachievers, have learning disabilities, and/or belong to under-represented populations such as the economically disadvantaged and racial/ethnic/linguistic/cultural minority groups. For these reasons, for years educators have advocated using multiple assessment instruments and practices. Another factor is staff development: Teachers trained in gifted education provide more effective instruction to gifted students. A school/program's teachers of gifted students should have certifications/endorsements in gifted education, and schools should provide regular in-service trainings regarding gifted students. Because gifted students are different from other students, schools also should provide guidance services to address problems such as fitting in socially with non-gifted peers and gifted hypersensitivities to the ordinary stresses of growing up and attending school. Additionally, schools should confer equivalent honors to academic talents/achievements as to athletic talents/achievements.

Any good gifted education program or school should state its learning outcome expectations clearly for the student. Providing activities that students enjoy is important, but gifted students also must learn while having fun. Specifying learning objectives and designing instruction to facilitate reaching those objectives is an essential part of any gifted program. Gifted education programs/schools should provide curricula that stimulate and challenge their students. Gifted students often grow bored if instructional tasks are too easy and do not require them to "stretch" their minds. Flexibility is important to help gifted students receive suitable challenges and meet individual needs. For example, students who perform several years above grade level in one subject should not be made to do grade-level work. Programs should be flexible to let such students study higher-level material. Students with musical gifts could exchange some school time for participation in special music programs, or study with an "artist-teacher" musician.

Program management

Educational researchers have observed that in some gifted programs, little time and few resources are left for the crucial components of curriculum design, program evaluation, and staff development, because so much time and effort are disproportionately devoted to the identification of gifted students. Nonetheless, researchers have clarified that this observation reflects not a criticism of program managers but instead an insight about the unrealistic expectations and insufficient investment in quality programs for students with high ability. Because trends increasingly emphasize curriculum planning and student assessment for such quality programs, greater program management capacities are needed. Progress includes greater recognition and provision of a variety of service options at the program level to meet diverse student and community needs, program developers' responses to the National Association for Gifted Children's standards for conveying program expectations, and the positive perceptions by constituents of the quality of staff in good gifted programs.

Recent issues and trends

Researchers in gifted education have identified issues in some gifted programs that reflect common concerns in gifted education. Programs including part-time pull-outs, cluster grouping within general education classrooms, and center-based gifted programs all share some common concerns. Even with well-established, exemplary curriculum units, a need exists to reconsider the organization and focus relative to progress in cognitive learning theory and to content standards. The emphasis on documenting how instruction supports students' learning requires educators to consider differentiated instruction in greater depth. Performance-based assessments have gained greater prominence in evaluating learning because they are more congruent with higher-order content standards such as enabling more student demonstration of reasoning and problem-solving skills in specific subjects. Implications include that assessment must play a more central role in program and curriculum planning rather than depending only on traditional standardized achievement tests. Furthermore, collection and reporting of performance-based student impact data as well as more integration of assessment techniques and economy in analyzing data are indicated to promote both learning and accountability.

Program placement option with resource services

The term "resource services" refers to the student in the general education classroom going to a separate resource room part-time, also called pull-out program or send-out classes, available in some middle schools and more prevalent in elementary schools. Typically, groups of 10-30 students attend a resource room for classes with a gifted teacher for one day or ½ day weekly. Gifted teachers may reserve one weekday for third-graders, and designate two other days for cross-grade groups of fourth- and fifth- and/or fifth- and sixth-graders in the resource room. They might visit regular classrooms to teach model lessons on a fourth weekday, and use the fifth day for completing their administrative duties.

Implementing a pull-out/resource room

One less common, but valuable, way to implement a pull-out program is with a multiple-year curriculum, which affords continuity. For example, using the theme of change and adaptation, fourth-graders could study environmental changes; fifth-graders could examine political changes under oligarchies, monarchies, and democracies; and sixth-graders could learn of changing family roles in different regions of our country. Another method involves extending the regular classroom curriculum by studying the same subjects or topics in more depth. A third approach is basing the pull-out curriculum on national or regional enrichment programs, e.g. Odyssey of the Mind, Science Olympiad, or the Future Problem-Solving Program, and adding activities focused on the underlying reasoning and creative skills whereby students succeed in such programs. In a fourth approach, the resource-room gifted teacher decides the pull-out curriculum. In this case, the quality of program content depends largely on the knowledge, experience, and skills of the individual teacher.

Advantages and disadvantages of a school's using a pull-out or resource services program

Pull-out programs give gifted students the benefits of weekly classroom interactions with their intellectual peers and of sharing experiences involving their individual strengths. Many gifted students look forward to this so much that they will never miss school on their pull-out day. Pull-out classes often have open-ended enough curricula to allow freedom of creative exploration, enlisting the teachers' and students' skills and imaginations to design projects of interest and value, which is another advantage. Having gifted resource-room teachers is also financially advantageous to school districts, as these teachers usually work with all gifted students at various grade levels, teach lessons in regular classrooms, conduct in-service trainings for other teachers and staff, field parents' phone calls as delegated by their school principals, and perform other functions entailing intensive communication with varied audiences.

One disadvantage of pull-out programs is that school personnel may not adequately coordinate their activities with the regular classroom curriculum. Consequently some teachers—and students—wonder how some pull-out activities relate to general education subjects. Another problem occurs if resource teachers base projects on their own interests rather than students' strengths. Many teacher resources are available for activities supporting higher levels of learning, but teachers often do not avail themselves of these curriculum guides and materials. The activities they design for gifted students should not only be fun and interesting for the students, but also develop their advanced cognitive

skills. Rarely, some general classroom teachers resent gifted students' weekly absence and retaliate by scheduling class parties or field trips, important tests, and/or new topic introductions on pull-out days. This unprofessional behavior is uncommon but problematic. Also, some busy classroom teachers do not give gifted students other differentiated learning choices for the rest of the week, mistakenly thinking the pull-out program is enough.

Expense of gifted pull-out programs vs. inclusive, regular classroom-based gifted instruction

Suppose that a school district has two schools served by a gifted resource teacher. A total of 60 gifted students are served, with 30 gifted students in each school. Each school has two classrooms per grade, and the gifted students are in second through fifth grades. Four grades x two classrooms = eight, x two schools = 16. With pull-out programs, the resource teacher can teach one group of students per grade level, or four groups at each school (eight total). The teacher can do this in two full school days, one at each school. In contrast, if this teacher had to go to sixteen separate regular classrooms to teach the gifted students, it would take more time, and that time would be more fragmented. The teacher likely could not see students as regularly. Researchers found when a school district switched from pull-out to in-class programs, it cost three times as much to hire three times as many specialists as they had needed with pull-out teaching.

Remediating some of the drawbacks of pull-out/resource room programs

To remedy a lack of coordination between pull-out activities and regular classroom curriculum, the resource teacher can circulate a newsletter to classroom teachers explaining their resource room activities and how they connect with the regular curriculum. To provide both gifted resource teachers and general classroom teachers with reciprocal insights into each other's work and experiences, they can each trade places for a day or half-day. The gifted resource teacher can offer to teach a lesson for the regular classroom teacher, who can observe the teaching strategies the resource teacher uses for gifted as well as regular students. The gifted resource teacher also can propose that the two teachers work together to team-teach a regular class that includes gifted students. Educational researchers find that pull-out programs can succeed or fail depending on whether or not the regular and gifted teachers share mutual understanding, solid communication, and positive interactions.

Placement option for gifted students consisting of a self-contained "special education" program

Self-contained gifted classes consist entirely of gifted students. In districts having these, they are at the elementary school level. If middle and high school students are placed in each subject via ability grouping, these classes may function as self-contained. However, true self-contained gifted classes for all subjects do not exist in regular public secondary schools due to subject departmentalization. Advantages include the ability to design more gifted-appropriate instruction overall; higher gifted student achievement levels than those in pull-out gifted programs; usually no extra expense, as the gifted class will have the same number of students as a regular class at that grade level; the greater ability of gifted students to relate to their intellectual peers; and a more supportive classroom atmosphere, more conducive to freedom of expression and more encouraging relative to individual student strengths and weaknesses, which

allows gifted students to perform better and more consistently.

Disadvantages of a school's having self-contained classes for the gifted

One disadvantage of self-contained gifted classes that continue for several years is that gifted students lack classroom interactions with non-gifted peers. One solution is to have activities such as lunch, physical education, art, and music include all students to provide interaction. Some school districts create "teams" of several classrooms, including the self-contained gifted class, so gifted and other students interact daily. Another problem occurs when either too few or too many gifted students are identified for the school's normal class size. A smaller gifted class would provoke resentment in teachers with normal, larger class sizes; a group too large would force schools to leave out some qualified gifted students. Self-contained classes also can lead to student, teacher, and parent perceptions of school elitism and isolationism. Also, though there is no proof that other students suffer, some teachers still feel that removing the gifted students leaves the other students with no role models.

Cluster grouping

One practice that schools employ to meet the educational needs of their gifted students is to use cluster grouping. This practice entails grouping all of the gifted children at one grade level inclusively in one regular classroom. For example, if a school has three separate fourth-grade classrooms and a total of six fourth-graders identified as gifted, these students would all be placed in one of those classrooms rather than being distributed among several fourth-grade classrooms. This works for students gifted in individual subjects; a student with verbal gifts can be in a different classroom than a student with mathematical gifts. Some benefits are that cluster grouping is inexpensive and that students can move fluidly in and out of cluster groups. A drawback of cluster grouping is that globally gifted students cannot attend multiple classrooms simultaneously to meet their advanced needs in multiple subjects. Another consideration is that teachers must differentiate their instruction for greater variations in ability levels within one class.

Collaborative consultative model

The collaborative consultative model of education posits three component entities: the Consultant, the Mediator (the consultee), and the Target (usually the student). This model views the consultant and consultee as equal partners. They bring varying expertise to the collaboration and have mutual responsibility for identifying problems, planning strategies for interventions, and carrying out recommendations through combining their respective knowledge and skills. Disagreements between consultant and consultee are regarded as constructive opportunities to extract the most helpful information. This model assumes that consultant and consultee will both work directly with the target or student. Educational researchers have found in surveying teachers that while time shortages and scheduling issues can interfere with the success of collaborative consultative services, most teachers find them acceptable as alternatives to resource room services; furthermore, some teachers find them very desirable as alternatives. This model addresses special student needs, including giftedness as well as disabilities.

Advantages and disadvantages of the collaborative consultative model

One of the benefits of using collaborative consultative models in gifted education involves the congruence of such models with recent trends in educational reform. Another benefit affords professional development for all those participating as they contribute and share their expertise. Collaboration also allows many more ideas to be produced than any individual could generate in isolation. In addition, consultative methods make the most of the opportunity for the adult participants to use their individual differences toward achieving constructive goals. Another advantage of the collaborative consultative model is that it is amenable to the school administrator's taking the role of facilitator. Moreover, using collaboration and consultation between teachers, parents, and others from outside of the school affords the benefit of parents' satisfaction through their direct involvement, contributions, learning from others, and seeing their children's knowledge and social skills improve.

While there are many definite advantages for using the collaborative consultative model to meet students' special needs, including those of gifted students, there are also a few potential issues to consider. First, teachers, parents, and other participants from outside the school may have little or no training collaboration, unless the school institutes such training. If the school does so, another consideration is the time, expense, and human energy involved in providing training. Another very real consideration is that any or all of the potential collaborators may not have sufficient time to interact with one another. In addition, some educators prefer working with students, and would rather not work with other adults, especially if they lack relevant experiences. Moreover, implementation of collaborative

Copyright © Mometrix Media. You have been licensed one copy of this document for personal use only. Any other reproduction or redistribution is strictly prohibited. All rights reserved.

consultative methods requires firm support from the school administrator. Finally, while collaborative consultation is effective, visible results take time, so patience is needed.

Primary value of self-contained classes for gifted students

The primary value of self-contained classes for gifted students is the academic rigor possible when all students in a class are at similar intellectual levels. The general classroom teacher will not have to differentiate instruction specifically for gifted students by offering more in-depth study of subject content, materials at higher grade levels for acceleration, compacted curriculum, alternative activities, etc., if no gifted students are present. However, one inherent pitfall is that some general education teachers, relieved of the necessity to differentiate instruction for gifted students, may fail to differentiate instruction for their existing students. Such failure reflects that these teachers do not understand (or observe) that differentiation is intended to customize teaching for the needs of every individual student, not just every individual gifted student. Varying difficulty levels, paces, prior knowledge, interests, and learning styles also require differentiation among non-gifted students.

Ability grouping

Ability grouping should not be equated or confused with cluster grouping, heterogeneous grouping, or tracking. Ability grouping involves dividing the students within one classroom and grouping them according to their ability levels, which can differ broadly within one general education classroom. This grouping by ability is not rigid but fluid, and it can be changed as needed at any time. For example, a student might be placed into a high ability group for math and participate in a group of middle ability for reading. If that student's reading improves, the student could move into the high ability group for reading. Conversely, if a student develops problems in an individual subject, s/he can move into a lower ability group to address his or her academic needs best. The flexibility of ability grouping allows gifted students more options to receive the most appropriate instruction and to adjust for needs that change over time.

Independent study

Independent study gives gifted students encouragement and preparation for initiating, implementing, and successfully completing their own scholastic activities in their areas of interest. As such, it provides them with a structural context for making choices and decisions about what and how they learn. It also teaches them how to communicate what they have learned. When gifted students have independent study projects, these also benefit teachers by helping them to fulfill the roles of facilitating students' progress, listening to students, and clarifying ideas and objectives. Many gifted students underachieve; this can be related to lack of interest in assigned topics, frustration at not being able to study subjects in more depth, boredom with the mainstream class pace and/or types of assignments. Independent study of a topic a student is passionate about can alleviate these factors and increase task commitment. Planning and executing projects stimulates inquiry, builds motivation and self-discipline, improves study skills and habits, and promotes positive attitudes and self-concepts.

Participating in an independent study program

Teachers should ensure that any independent study program for a gifted student will meet their individual instructional needs as well as their particular personal interests. In self-selected studies, the gifted student chooses a topic s/he wants to study that will meet these needs and interests. In related studies or "spin-off" studies, the gifted student is acquainted with a subject in the usual teacher-directed class lessons, and then selects a topic within that subject that particularly interests her/him to investigate in more depth and specificity through an independent study project. In curricular studies, the teacher will have made a list of topics based on the subject content for the whole class to study. Gifted students can select one topic from this teacher-made list and conduct an independent study of it. Curricular topics may be studied independently by individual gifted students; or they may also collaborate on these in small group settings.

Online information about community resources

Many websites offer information on community resources for gifted and talented students. One good resource is the website of the National Association for Gifted Children (NAGC). State associations can join NAGC as an affiliate. State affiliates then can offer NAGC Parent Affiliate Memberships to parents of gifted children. On the NAGC website, there is a Gifted by State page. As of its 2008 copyright, it linked to organizations for every U.S. state except Alaska and Wyoming. Minnesota has two gifted organizations linked. Websites of state organizations for the gifted offer such information as local chapters, publications, webinars, audio recordings, upcoming events, recent news; the organization's mission statement; the state's definition of giftedness; programming standards; legislative updates; summer teacher professional development courses, workshops, institutes, conferences, etc.; e-stores;

awards and scholarships; communicators; advocacy information; job postings; and more. State gifted organizations' sites also list and link to local community resources within their state, including other gifted associations; college/university programs; academic/enrichment opportunities including competitions, activities, programs, and journals.

Positive outcomes of independent study

Independent study projects allow gifted students to explore a variety of subjects and areas in which they are interested. Planning, developing, and carrying out an independent study project can serve as the student's introduction to the methods used to organize, research, and present the results obtained to others.   With guidance and support from teachers, independent study can encourage gifted students to develop individual qualities of initiative as well as their intellectual and creative abilities. Independent study activities stimulate gifted students' skills in critical thinking, logical reasoning, and continuity in focus. By working on independent study projects, gifted students develop a sense of personal responsibility for pursuing their goals. In addition, when they pursue and successfully attain their goals through independent study, gifted students attain a sense of satisfaction and achievement.

Conducting an independent study project

The gifted student chooses a topic of special interest and reads extensively about it, developing a knowledge base. With a general grasp of the topic and knowing what s/he wants to discover, the student asks questions to answer. Students utilize and develop higher-order cognitive skills as they learn to identify and use resources in the forms of places and persons, establish goals and objectives, develop and carry out plans to accomplish these, make self-evaluations of their own work, and identify avenues whereby they can communicate their discoveries, conclusions, and knowledge. Students can use fact cards to record information they collect on the topic. By analyzing the information they gather, students can develop questions reflecting a problem to solve; for example, the student can ask what methods s/he could use to get a specific species of wildlife off the endangered list. This process demands student analysis of information, creation of novel and unusual plans, and expression of their opinions. It also involves them in authentic research, products, and audiences.

One category of research that gifted students can use for independent study is historical research, which endeavors to reconstruct the past objectively. Some sources for gathering information include old newspapers, written records, oral history, baby books, folk songs, poems, and stories. Students could study the history of the school, the community; some aspect of the U.S. Constitution or Bill of Rights, etc. Another category is developmental research, which examines trends, change, continuity, sequences, and patterns. Developmental psychology and human growth and development are examples of developmental research areas. Students can investigate such topics as human biological development, cognitive development in children, personality development over the lifespan, etc. Another category is descriptive research, which is quantitative. Numerical statistics are depicted using graphs, charts, and tables. Students can conduct opinion or fact-finding surveys, or observational or interview studies.

Experimental research

In experimental research, the researcher seeks to discover whether one variable causes changes in another variable. Statistical methods of multivariate analysis can also be applied to study the effects of and on multiple variables within the same experiment or set of experiments. For example, gifted students use independent study projects to research whether a plant responds differentially to various stimuli or which combinations of substances will produce a certain chemical reaction. Experimental studies involving human subjects include such research questions as whether the amount of sleep the night before an exam affects student test performance, whether one school curriculum is more conducive to student motivation than another, or whether internal or external rewards have greater positive influences on student performance. Experimenters establish a treatment group receiving the intervention being tested, and a control group receiving no treatment to control for extraneous variables. By manipulating the independent variable being tested, researchers can see if it affects the selected dependent variable(s).

Gifted education and special education

Many students with gifts in specific areas and/or global giftedness also have disabilities. This complicates the circumstances of the best educational programming for them. One consideration is that disabilities can prevent some gifted students from being identified as gifted. For example, if a student has visual impairment and does not receive appropriate classroom accommodations, it might not be discovered that this student also has superior language and reading abilities. Another consideration is that instruction must be differentiated in certain ways to accommodate the needs of students with disabilities, and in other ways to accommodate the needs of gifted and talented students. The challenge for educators is to combine and coordinate both types of differentiation for these doubly/multiply exceptional students. An additional aspect is that federal laws exist to guarantee education to disabled students but not to gifted students. Therefore, many U.S. state regulations for gifted education are modeled upon federal laws protecting the rights of disabled students.

One factor important to consider in both gifted education and general education, since it affects both, is that compared to the numbers of special schools for gifted and talented students, there are many more public schools attended by gifted and talented students. Additionally, while some public schools include self-contained classes composed entirely of identified gifted and talented students, many more have such students mainstreamed into general education classrooms along with non-gifted students. Many public schools have pull-out programs for gifted students wherein they attend resource rooms to participate in special, individualized activities with instruction from a gifted education teacher. However, pull-out programs only involve a portion of the students' school time, typically a half-day or one day at most. Therefore, it is crucial for general and gifted education teachers to coordinate their curricula and activities. Each must know what the other is doing to facilitate the student's educational progress.

Correlational research

Correlational research is a type of quantitative research method that compares quantitative data obtained to discover whether a relationship exists between two or more variables. Specifically, it seeks to find whether one variable affects another variable and how. A positive correlation means that as one variable increases or decreases in amount or number, so does the other variable. A negative or inverse correlation means that as one variable increases, the other decreases, and vice versa. Statistics also show the strength of the correlation, or the degree of relationship. Some examples include whether the seasons affect school attendance, whether an individual's head size and foot size are related, or whether school attendance affects achievement test scores. Correlations do not imply causations: two variables may increase or decrease together or oppositely, but this does not mean that either variable causes the other. To determine causation, experimental research must be used.

Program evaluation and assessment

Evaluation plans are crucial elements in the provision of services and programs for gifted students. Formative evaluations are made during the implementation of a program for educators to see that their programs accomplish their intended goals. Summative evaluations are made following full program implementation to assess the extent to which the program attains its goals and objectives. To enable both formative and summative assessment of a gifted education program, the element of evaluation should be built into the original program plan. A common error made in some programs involves waiting to plan the evaluation until the program has been in use for a year or two. Educators may wait this period in order to ensure their program is fully implemented prior to assessment, but planning should be done initially to allow both formative and summative assessments and to assure that the services offered can be evaluated in both these ways.

Conducting program evaluations

Some of the guidelines given by the National Research Center on the Gifted and Talented for program evaluation involve the following. In program development, educators should incorporate evaluation procedures into the earliest planning stages. They should develop a specific plan for how they will use their evaluation results. They should use multiple sources such as students, teachers, parents, administrators, and school board members, for information to develop clear program goals and descriptions. They should allow enough time and funds for evaluations. They must also prepare/train their school staff to conduct assessments and analyze the results. Educators should identify clearly all parties needing, and/or interested in, evaluation findings, and engage them in the process of evaluation. Because the results of gifted education programs are complex, educators must find or create appropriate assessment instruments. Data collection methods should reflect the organization and objectives of gifted programs, e.g. portfolio assessments, out-of-level testing, product ratings with inter-rater reliability, etc. Educators should report evaluation findings timely to all those involved, including follow-up recommendations.

Purpose of program evaluation

An important reason to evaluate gifted programs is to ascertain whether the school's/educators' implementation of their program is congruent with their initial program plans and/or to what degree. To determine this, they can examine: identification of gifted/talented students, services provided to them, data available showing how effective their screening/identification systems are, criteria for screening and identification to prevent overlooking special populations, available curriculum options for meeting student academic needs, data available showing how effective the curriculum is, whether/how acceleration is used, how effective their acceleration options are, how program goals and objectives are implemented, how these are connected to district philosophy and mission statements, impacts of the program on the regular education program(s), opportunities available for advanced training to all teachers, how formal and informal feedback is used for program quality improvement, student educational outcomes, curriculum approach implementation at different grade levels, and evidence showing the value of current service delivery models.

Applying Leadership and Communication Skills to Support Gifted and Talented Students

Resources available for professional development and learning

- Professional literature - books and publications are examples of literature that can help a classroom teacher.
- Colleagues - a fellow member of a profession, staff, or academic faculty; an associate
- Professional Associations - an association of practitioners of a given profession, for example NEA, NSTA, etc.
- Professional development activities – sometimes put on by a local or state school board to teach educators the newest trends in education.

Code of Ethics

Ethical codes are specialized and specific rules of ethics. Such codes exist in most professions to guide interactions between specialists with advanced knowledge, e.g., doctors, lawyers and engineers, and the general public. They are often not part of any more general theory of ethics but accepted as pragmatic necessities. Ethical codes are distinct from moral codes that apply to the education and religion of a whole larger society. Not only are they more specialized, but they are more internally consistent, and typically can be applied without a great deal of interpretation by an ordinary practitioner of the specialty.

School as a resource to the larger community

Our mission is to work with communities to ensure learner success and stronger communities through family-school-community partnerships. Through schools, individuals value learning; learn how to learn; demonstrate effective communication, thinking and problem solving; enjoy a better quality of life; are fulfilled; experience the joy of learning; and contribute to and benefit from the intergenerational transmission of culture. in supporting the educational role and function of local education agencies (and organizations), families, and communities increase local capacity to improve and ensure learning opportunities for the children and citizens of the community.

Advocating for learners

Public support for education is fragile. Poverty jeopardizes the well-being and education of our young people and some communities are caught in a downward spiral of cynicism and mistrust. Teachers must necessarily be advocates for education. One might become involved in efforts to change policies, programs, and perceptions to benefit learners; such involvement is crucial for educators today, for when they do not create effective channels of communication with legislators, the media, and community members, their opinions will very likely go unfulfilled legislatively. These consequences can be devastating to children and to learning. The stakes are simply too high for educators not to engage in advocacy efforts. Just as teaching and learning require commitment, energy, and perseverance, so too does advocacy.

Parental education

As families shrank during the last half of the past century, parental education rose.

Among adolescents ages 12-17 in 1940, about 70% had parents who had completed no more than 8 years of school, while only 15% had parents who were high school graduates, and 3% had parents who were college graduates. Expenditures for education have expanded enormously since then, and the educational attainment figures have been turned on their head. By 2000, only 6% of adolescents ages 12-17 have parents with no more than 8 years of school, while 82% have parents with high school diplomas, including the 21%-29% who have mothers or fathers with 4-year college degrees.

Parental educational attainment is perhaps the most central feature of family circumstances relevant to overall child well-being and development, regardless of race/ethnicity or immigrant origins. Parents who have completed fewer years of schooling may be less able to help their children with schoolwork because of their limited exposure to knowledge taught in the classroom. They also may be less able to foster their children's educational success in other ways because they lack familiarity with how to negotiate educational institutions successfully. Children whose parents have extremely limited education may, therefore, be more likely to benefit from, or to require, specialized educational program initiatives if their needs are to be met by educational institutions.

Parents with limited educational attainment may also be less familiar with how to access successfully social institutions, such as healthcare, with which children and their parents must interact in order to receive needed services. Equally important is that parent educational attainment influences their income levels. Parents with limited education tend to command lower wages in the labor market and are, therefore, constrained in the educational, health,

and other resources that they can afford to purchase for their children. For all of these reasons, among children generally, negative educational and employment outcomes have been found for children with low parental educational attainment.

Student diversity

Cultural identities are strongly embraced by adolescents but they also want to be recognized and treated as unique individuals. Teachers walk a fine line between respecting cultural differences and avoiding overly emphasizing them or disregarding them altogether. Responding to discriminatory comments immediately, using a wide variety of examples, quoting scholars from many cultures and identifying universal problems needing complex solutions can indirectly communicate appreciation of and respect for all cultures. Teachers must take care never to imply any kind of stereotype or make comments that might indicate a cultural bias. They must refrain from asking a student to respond as a member of a particular culture, class or country. Teachers should learn as much as they can about every racial, ethnic and cultural group represented in their classroom. It is also important that teachers respect students' commitments and obligations away from school, their family responsibilities and job pressures.

Cultural influences

Study after study has shown that a student's culture has a direct impact on learning. Since educational standards are based on white, middle class cultural identification, students who do not fall into that demographic face challenges every day. It's not that these students are incapable of learning; they simply judge that which is important and how they express that importance differently. Sometimes it is difficult for them to understand and relate to curriculum content, teaching methods and social skills required because their culture does things differently, emphasizes different choices and rewards different behavior. Adolescents identify with their culture; they become what they know. If teachers ignore cultural differences, it causes communication issues, inhibits learning and increases the potential for behavior problems. As long as a child has no physical or mental health issues, he is capable of learning. He simply needs that the information presented and examples used to be relevant to his life experiences; otherwise, it does not seem to make sense to him.

Social environment

The social environment is the set of people and institutions with which one associates and communicates. It has both a direct and indirect influence on behavior by the individuals within the group. It is sometimes defined by specific characteristics such as race, gender, age, culture or behavioral patterns. When defined by behavioral patterns it can lead to unproven assumptions about entire groups of people. In America's diverse society, it is essential that teachers recognize that various social groups exist within a classroom and thus determine the best strategies not only to facilitate the learning of "book" facts, but also to encourage understanding and acceptance between the groups. The learning theory called social cognitivism believes that people learn by observing others, whether they are aware of the process or not. Creating opportunities for students to interact with diverse social groups in a neutral, non-threatening situation can bring about positive interpersonal growth that could have long-term societal impact outside of the educational environment.

Socialization

Socialization is the process of learning the written and unwritten rules, acceptable behavioral patterns, and accumulated knowledge of the community in order to function within its culture. It is a gradual process that starts when a person is born and, in one form or another, continues throughout his life. There are many "communities" within a culture: e.g., family, school, neighborhood, military and country. There are six forms of socialization:

- Reverse Socialization: deviation from acceptable behavior patterns.
- Developmental Socialization: the process of learning social skills.
- Primary Socialization: learning the attitudes, values and actions of a culture.
- Secondary Socialization: learning behavior required in a smaller group within the culture.
- Anticipatory Socialization: practicing behavior in preparation for joining a group.
- Resocialization: discarding old behavior and learning new behavior as part of a life transition; e.g., starting school, moving to a new neighborhood or joining the military.

The agents of socialization are the people, groups and institutions that influence the self-esteem, emotions, attitudes, behavior and acceptance of a person within his environment. The first agents are the immediate family (mother, father, siblings) and extended family (grandparents, aunts, uncles, cousins). They influence religious affiliation, political inclinations, educational choices, career aspirations and other life goals. The school's role is explaining societal values, reinforcing acceptable behavior patterns and teaching necessary skills such as reading, writing, reasoning and critical thinking. Peer groups (people who are about the same age) share certain characteristics (attend the same school, live in the same neighborhood) and influence values, attitudes and behavior. The media (radio, television, newspapers, magazines, the Internet) have an impact on attitude, values and one's understanding of the activities of society and international events. Other institutions that influence people include religion, the work place, the neighborhood, and city, state and federal governments.

Social ineptitude

Social ineptitude is defined as a lack of social skills; in most societies, this term is considered disrespectful. There are medical conditions that may cause a deficiency in social skills such as autism and Asperger syndrome. Someone who believes himself socially inept may have an avoidant personality disorder. A shy person or an overly bold person may observe societal conventions but still exhibit social incompetence; the behavior is simply manifested in different ways. The criteria for social ineptitude are different in different cultures, which makes it difficult to cite specific examples. People trying to integrate into a new environment may unknowingly commit a social faux pas thereby earning the damaging label unfairly. In a culturally diverse classroom, it is critical to create an atmosphere of acceptance so if a student does something inappropriate, the behavior can be quietly and gently corrected without causing humiliation or embarrassment.

Social skills

Social skills are the tools used to interact and communicate with others. They are learned during the socialization process and are both verbal and non-verbal. These skills are integral to becoming an active and accepted member of any environment. There are general skills needed to complete daily transactions such as being able to ask sensible questions and provide logical answers and knowing how to read and write and understand simple directions. If these skills are missing or poorly executed, it can cause various problems and misunderstandings, some of which could have long-lasting and/or life-changing consequences. In smaller groups, other skills may be needed such as the ability to engage in interesting conversation, present ideas to peers, teach new concepts or actively participate in discussions. Using body language and gestures appropriate to the situation and the message, having the ability to resolve conflicts and being diplomatic when necessary are examples of advanced social skills.

Meeting with parents

Studies have shown that the more parents are involved in their children's education, the better the students learn and the fewer behavior problems one must handle. Teachers are an integral part of the process. It is up to them to keep parents informed about the academic and social progress of the students. Report cards only provide letter or number grades and are not designed to explore and explain how well the student is learning and progressing in the intangible skills like critical thinking, reasoning ability, study habits, attitude, communication with adults and peers and other social and interactive development. Sending home periodic progress reports is an effective way to keep parents abreast of changes. Meeting with parents regularly to discuss their child's particular progress and being available to answer questions are excellent ways to work together as a team to ensure the student benefits the most from his educational experience.

Parent/student/teacher agreement

If a teacher should wish to use a formal parent/student/teacher agreement as a way to involve parents, provide students with a written set of expectations and explain their commitment to a successful educational experience, there are several activities that can be included:

- Parent Priorities:
  - Show respect for and support of the student, teacher and the discipline policy.
  - Monitor homework assignments and projects.
  - Attend teacher conferences.
  - Ask about the student's day.
- Student Priorities:
  - Show respect for parents, teachers, peers and school property.
  - Put forth his best effort both in class and at home.
  - Come to class prepared.
  - Talk to his parents about school.
- Teacher Priorities:
  - Show respect for the student, his family and his culture.
  - Help each student strive to reach his potential.
  - Provide fair progress evaluations to students and parents.
  - Enforce rules fairly and consistently.

Many schools use some sort of parent/student/teacher agreement to ensure everyone understands the rules and agrees to abide by them. It can be as simple as requiring parents, students and teachers to sign a copy of the student handbook or it can be a formal contract drafted with specific activities each

pledges to perform. Whichever format is used, it should detail each party's responsibilities. This accomplishes several goals:

- Parents are recognized as an important part of the educational experience. They are also made aware of what is expected of them, their children, the teachers and the administration.
- Students are given written expectations, which prevent an "I didn't know" attitude. It encourages respect for himself, his parents, his teachers, his peers and the rules.
- Teachers make a written commitment to students and parents to provide an environment that encourages learning. They list specific, observable behavior which they pledge to perform.

Levels of parental involvement

Some parents are eager to participate in their child's education, some do so only when required, and others avoid involvement of any kind. All three approaches can be a challenge. Eager parents may bombard the teacher and administration with notes, phone calls, emails and requests for information and meetings. Setting reasonable, well-defined limits may be necessary. Parents who only show up when specifically requested (e.g., semi-annual parent/teacher conferences, meeting with the administration about a behavior problem), might only be going through the motions in order to keep their child enrolled in school. They may be incapable of or don't really care to address any underlying issues; they show up because they are required to do so. Parents who are never available and impossible to contact provide no help or insight and offer no support.

Parent/teacher conferences

Basics

Parent/teacher conferences can be stressful experiences for both parties. But with a positive attitude and much preparation, they can be pleasant, provide a forum for the exchange of information and improve the educational experience for the students. The first step is for the teacher to be rested. Fatigue can cause an inability to concentrate, unfortunate misunderstandings and inappropriate reactions. If a teacher thinks parents might be difficult to handle, it might be wise to ask an administrator to sit in. The teacher needs to have a plan prepared with discussion points and copies of the student's work available to review. He needs to keep in mind that the parents may have items to discuss as well, and therefore the plan needs to be flexible and allow time for questions. The discussion should focus on the positive and present negative information with a "we can fix it" approach.

In order to avoid wasting everyone's time during a parent/teacher conference, there are several things a teacher can do to set the scene for a productive meeting. Make initial contact early by sending a note or newsletter home briefly outlining plans and objectives for the year and providing contact information (e.g., phone number, email address, days and times available). This tells parents the teacher is willing to talk and/or meet when necessary. When a date for a conference is set, the teacher should be certain to invite both parents. It is the best way to gauge how involved they are, yet individual family circumstances need to be considered (one-parent families, parents' work commitments, et cetera). Schedule twenty to thirty minute conferences; if more time becomes necessary, schedule a follow-up meeting. Develop a flexible agenda and gather necessary paperwork. Verify parent and student names just before the meeting.

Encouraging parental involvement

Every teacher needs to develop ways in which to involve parents in the education of their children. Some communication methods may be more effective than others depending upon the age of the students, the educational level and time limitations of the parents, and the administrative support and resources available to the teacher. Some schools encourage a parent orientation program at the beginning of the year, in which the teacher informs parents what his expectations are concerning behavior and outlines classroom rules. He presents a broad picture of the material to be covered, projects that will be assigned and homework requirements. If a meeting isn't possible, the same information can be conveyed in a letter sent home just before school starts or during the first week. Besides regularly scheduled parent/teacher conferences, a periodic newsletter, perhaps when report cards are issued, can be sent to update parents.

Being prepared

Parent/teacher conferences are the best time for candid communication. For the encounter to be productive, both parties need to be prepared to discuss the student's strengths and weaknesses, share any concerns and decide upon the best way to help the student meet required goals and reach his potential. Some topics to consider in preparation for this important meeting:

- The skills and knowledge that should be learned and mastered.
- Required academic standards. Give parents a copy to which to refer during the year, and explain these standards. Projects planned and assignments required to complete academic requirements. The evaluation method, what data

is considered and when progress reports are issued. How parents can help. Suggest concrete activities which they can do at home in order to encourage learning and support the teacher's efforts. Programs available for both fast and slow learners. What programs are available to prepare students for life after high school.

Things to remember

Try to use a table rather than a desk and chairs so that the parents and the teacher meet as equals; this creates a more relaxed environment. Start with a positive statement about the student and then briefly review the objectives of the meeting. The teacher should not do all of the talking; it should be a conversation, not a monologue. Avoid educational jargon. Many parents will not understand it or will interpret it incorrectly. Focus on strengths, give specific examples, provide suggestions for improvement and refer to actions rather than character. For example: "Sam turned in his essay the day after it was due," instead of "Sam is irresponsible." Ask for parents' opinions and listen to their responses. Use body language that shows interest and concern and make eye contact. Do not judge the parents' attitude or behavior, and consider cultural differences. Briefly summarize the discussion and end with a positive comment or observation about the student.

Conclusion

If either the teacher or the parents feel that there is more to discuss or that a follow-up meeting is necessary for an update on progress made, a time can be scheduled before the parents leave. As soon as possible after the conversation while the details are fresh, the teacher should make notes of the general discussion and record any specific actions that he or the parents agreed to take as

well as the parents' attitude and willingness to offer support. Any private information and/or family issues which the parents shared should be kept in the strictest confidence. If a cooperative relationship is to be established, parents need to know that their family business will remain private. It is very important and even required in some states that teachers report any indication of or concerns about possible child abuse or endangerment to the authorities. All teachers and administrators need to be familiar with the pertinent statutes in their state.

Cooperating with colleagues

To be successful, a teacher must be constantly cooperating with and learning from colleagues. There are a number of ways to do this; one is to set up regular meetings with them. Many teachers are part of a team of teachers who instruct the same group of students, and these meetings will therefore already be in place. If this is not the case, however, teachers should try to set up frequent meetings with colleagues who either teach the same students or the same subject. These meetings should not be the equivalent of teacher's lounge gripe sessions, but instead should be forums in which new teaching methods can be discussed, teaching content can be coordinated, and basic plans of behavior management can be established.

Peer review programs for teachers

Another way in which a community of teachers can foster professional improvement is through peer review. In a peer review program, teachers observe one another and offer suggestions for improvement. This is especially helpful when it is done among teachers in the same grade level or subject. Another teacher who is fluent in French, for instance, would be a great resource for a non-French-speaking teacher helping new immigrants from West Africa. Of course, in order for this sort of program to work, there needs to be a spirit of collaboration and constructive criticism among the teachers. Unfortunately, school politics and competitiveness often poison the relationships between colleagues, and make it difficult to offer or accept well-meaning suggestions. The best peer review programs establish a specific protocol for criticism and encouragement.

Mentoring programs for teachers

Mentoring is another professional improvement program that can be extremely valuable to a teacher. In a mentoring program, experienced teachers develop relationships with beginning teachers. The schools that use these programs find that they are able to retain a larger proportion of their beginning teachers. When mentoring programs are not offered, new teachers should ask a veteran teacher to act as a mentor, as a mentor can provide guidance on any aspect of teaching, from classroom management to lesson plans. New teachers get the most out of the relationship if they consciously remain open to constructive criticism. A mentor should observe his or her mentee directly in the teacher's classroom, but the mentee should also keep a list of concerns and questions to bring to private meetings. Teachers who accept advice and are willing to see things from a different perspective will grow immeasurably from the mentoring experience.

Peer tutoring programs

Another way that teachers can join with their colleagues in order to improve the quality of instruction is through peer tutoring. In a basic peer tutoring program, more advanced students work with the younger students on class work.

For instance, the members of a second-grade class might be paired with the members of a fifth-grade class. The older children will still be using many of the concepts that they learned in second grade, thus it will be beneficial for them to explain and demonstrate these concepts. The younger children, meanwhile, will enjoy working with older children and may be more receptive to the material when it comes from a source other than the teacher.

Peer tutoring relationships are especially fruitful when they are between students from similar backgrounds. In a modern class, there may be students from several different linguistic backgrounds. Some students may be the sole representative of their native culture in their grade level. If there are other students in the school with the same origin, however, they may be profitably united through peer tutoring. Also, peer tutoring programs are a great chance for students to develop their social skills; the older children will practice being generous and considerate of someone younger, while the younger children will practice being attentive and receptive to counsel. Of course, only those older students who have a good grasp of the content and are well-behaved should be involved in a peer tutoring program.

Field trips with other classes

Another way that teachers can band together is by arranging field trips with other teachers, as it is often easier to handle the logistics of a large field trip in cooperation with another teacher. Also, many field trips will have applications to multiple subject areas. For instance, a trip to a local battlefield could have relevance for American history, English, and Social Studies students. A visit to the local natural science museum could be pertinent to content in math, science, and history. It is always a good idea to encourage students to make associations between content areas. Furthermore, a field trip encourages students to mix with other students, forming social connections that improve investment in the academic setting.

Coordinating subject matter

One of the most positive ways for teachers to work with their fellow teachers is by coordinating subject matter. This strategy is often used in teacher "teams" in elementary and middle school, but it can also be effective in high school. Let us consider a brief example of how teachers can coordinate subject matter with great results. Imagine that you are a sixth-grade teacher. Before the school year begins, you could propose that the sixth grade uses "cities" as a theme. Each teacher can then construct lessons in their instructional domain that connect with this theme. As the teacher, you could look at texts that focus on life in the city. The history teacher could teach students about the rise of the big urban centers during the Industrial Revolution. The math teacher could incorporate some study of the various statistics and charts that are used to describe and learn about cities. If your school is located in or near a large city, you might also take some field trips so students can observe first-hand the things that they have learned.

Coordinating instructional content

The net effect of coordinating content seems to be that students learn more. Educational research suggests that all knowledge is associative, and people therefore tend to remember those things that they can easily fit into their existing store of information. If a teacher and his colleagues can link diverse disciplines together by looking at the same subject from a number of different perspectives, they can help students develop a well-rounded and coherent way of intellectually exploring the world. This is especially true for students, who will be encountering a dizzying amount of new information at school. If this material is disconnected and seemingly random, students will be more likely to forget it. Thematic content in multiple subjects helps avoid this problem.

Communicating with colleagues

An instructor should meet with his colleagues at some point during the year so that he can get a general idea of the structure and content of his colleague's classes. During the year, the teacher should stay abreast of that which students are learning in their other classes, and should note associations between disciplines whenever they arise. A teacher should also know when his fellow teachers are assigning major projects or exams, so that he can avoid giving important assignments on the same day. Many schools assign a certain day of the week for tests in each subject; e.g., math tests on Monday, history tests on Tuesday, and so on. If the school does not do this, the teacher should make sure that major projects and examinations are scheduled such that students are not overwhelmed with a flurry of work.

Relationship with school administration

It is important for the teacher to have a strong relationship with the school administration. The principals and support staff of a school are supposed to be there to make life easier, but they can only do this with cooperation. In order to maintain a happy partnership with the school administration, teachers should remember one guideline of great importance: namely, teachers should always report any significant problems immediately; these problems can include disciplinary matters, personal problems, or conflict with school protocol. In large schools where there is little one-on-one contact between the administration and the faculty, it is common for teachers to let their grievances fester in silence. The result is that what could be a cooperative relationship becomes poisoned by resentment and frustration. Teachers who have complaints or concerns about the way the school is being run, or who need help, should immediately discuss the problem with the principal.

Meeting with the principal

A teacher should try to avoid only visiting the principal when there is something wrong. A principal, like any person, will develop certain assumptions about a teacher whom they only see in times of crisis. Also, many principals will resent those teachers who they feel are constantly passing their problems onto the administration. Teachers should be referring problems to the principal only as a last resort. It is appropriate to let the principal know about concerns without necessarily asking for help. A teacher should try to check in with the principal periodically when things are going well in class, so that he or she can get a more balanced appreciation of the class' progress. When a teacher maintains a good relationship with the principal throughout the year, he or she will be much more helpful on those occasions of crisis.

Scheduling an observation by the principal

One great way to cultivate a positive relationship with the principal is to invite him or her to sit in on a class. A teacher should invite the principal on a day when a particularly innovative and exciting lesson is planned. It is a good idea to let the students know ahead of time that the principal will be joining the class, so they need to be on their best behavior. During the observation, the teacher should invite the principal to participate whenever appropriate. Many principals were teachers at one time, and will welcome the opportunity to join in with the activities of the class. After the class, the teacher should ask the principal for his opinion. As in relationships with other teachers, teachers should try to remain open to criticism and accepting of advice. These kinds of observations can be very useful for beginning teachers, who may be unaware of some fundamental mistakes they are making.

Relationships with teacher aides and assistants

Some teachers are lucky enough to have full- or part-time aides and assistants. When this is the case, the teacher should make sure that the aide is being used appropriately. For the most part, an aide should not be busy doing paperwork during class time. It is certainly useful to have another person to help with grading, but this can be done during the planning period or lunch. While the children are in the classroom, the aide should be another set of eyes and ears. In other words, the aide should circulate around the room while students are working. He can answer any questions students may have about the lesson, and can make sure that students stay on-task. Aides are also useful when some members of the class have fallen behind the others. The aide can assemble those students and give them a brief refresher on the recent material as the teacher instructs the rest of the class.

Frequent updates to parents

After sending this first letter home, it is also helpful to send home periodic notes letting parents know how the class is proceeding. If one has a small number of students, one may even be able to make personal phone calls to each parent.

Another way to stay in contact with many parents is through email; if one finds that all (or even some) of the parents in ones class have internet access, one may send out a short weekly update. Whatever format one chooses, one should try to keep parents informed of upcoming evaluations, field trips, and special events. If possible, one should personalize each message with some specific information about the child; this will convey the impression that one is taking a direct interest in the educational progress of each member of the class. It is important to make an effort to communicate both good news as well as bad. For many parents, the only contact they ever have with the school is when their child has gotten into trouble. One should occasionally make a call or drop a note to praise a student for improved academic performance. Parents will respond very positively to teachers who take the time to praise their children.

Keeping parents alert to student performance

It is also important to let parents know how their children are faring in class by sending home their grades regularly. Many teachers require students to take home their major tests and have them signed by a parent. Increasingly, teachers are posting student grades on a class website so that parents and students alike can keep track. Whichever method one chooses, one should make sure that one does not wait until the end of the term to let a parent know that their student is in danger of failing. As soon as any student falls behind, it is imperative to alert his parents so that a strategy for improvement can be developed. Do not assume that students will keep their parents informed as to how they are doing in class. Many students will claim to be doing well even if they know that this will be disproved by their final grade.

As a teacher, it is ones responsibility to keep parents informed.

Parent-teacher conferences

Another important part of developing a positive rapport with parents is the parent-teacher conference. Most elementary schools schedule these near the beginning of the year, often at the end of the first grading period. In middle and high school, parent-teacher conferences are not always mandatory, though they are recommended. If one is a beginning teacher, one may approach ones first conferences with some anxiety. It is important to remember, however, that both the teacher and the parent both have the student's success as a goal. It is important to accurately communicate a student's standing within the class. It is also important for both parties to agree on a strategy for maintaining or improving the student's performance subsequent to the conference. Conferences are meant to be punishment for neither the instructor, the parent, nor the student.

Teacher-parent phone call

When a student is struggling, contacting his parents should not be a last resort. Rather, it should be done soon so that the student's course can be corrected. Many students act out at school because of problems they are having at home; learning about these motivating factors can not only help one understand the behavior, but can lead to possible solutions. In any case, when one calls a parent to communicate bad news, it is important to always maintain a focus on the steps that should be taken for improvement. Do not call a parent simply to gripe. At the end of the call, make plans to talk again in the near future, so that everyone can assess how the strategy for improvement is proceeding. Always treat the parent as part of a team whose aim is the success of the student.

Open house

Another traditional means of making contact with parents is the open house. Most schools hold an open house at the beginning of the year so that parents can meet the teachers and see the classrooms. Besides being an opportunity to give information about the class, the open house is a chance for the teacher to present himself in a favorable light. The neatness and organization of the room is very important, as is greeting the parents as they enter. One should try to avoid getting bogged down in discussion with any one parent; discussions of individual students should be handled in another setting. The open house is a chance for one to sell oneself and the class. One should demonstrate the structure of one's class as well as present an appeal for help from parents.

Inviting parents to class

Besides the open house, parents should be invited to school whenever their presence will have a positive impact on learning. For instance, if students are going to be putting on a group or individual presentation, parents should be invited to attend. This is especially important in elementary grades, where the presence of a parent can be extremely comforting and motivating to students. Other instances where parents could be invited to attend school are field days, class parties, and field trips. Too often, students create a rigid separation between their school and home lives. Language differences reinforce this separation. By inviting parents to class, a teacher breaks down the division between the academic and the family life, and encourages the student to

incorporate what he is learning into all phases of his life.

Incorporating parents into instruction

A teacher should try to take advantage of parents' special skills or talents, especially as they relate to different content areas. For instance, if one is teaching a science-related unit and one of the students' parents is a botanist, you should invite him to speak to the class. If one is teaching a unit on Social Studies and discovers that one of the parents works for the federal government, it might be useful to invite him to speak. Whenever possible, one should be striving to make course content relevant to the daily lives of the students. There is no better way to do this than by incorporating their family members into the lesson.

Practice Test

Practice Questions

1. According to the Javits Act, gifted and talented students are described as those who:
   a. Have been assessed as having intelligence at least 30% above the national average, and are not receiving services or activities to develop those capabilities
   b. Are in the top 5% of their age group in terms of intellectual, creative, artistic, or leadership areas, or in specific academic fields
   c. Have achieved high accomplishment in intellectual, creative, artistic, or leadership areas or in specific academic fields, and who have not been recognized and honored in an appropriate manner
   d. Have the capability for high accomplishment in intellectual, creative, artistic, or leadership areas or in specific academic fields, and who need services or activities not ordinarily provided by the school to develop those capabilities

2. Gifted children typically get similar results with different types of I.Q. tests, such as the Wechsler Preschool and Primary Scale of Intelligence (WPPSI), the Stanford-Binet Intelligence Scale (SB), and the Wechsler Intelligence Scale for Children (WISC).
   a. Neither true nor false
   b. False
   c. True
   d. These I.Q. tests are not given to gifted students

3. Binh is in fifth grade. He was identified as gifted in leadership in third grade and entered into a Gifted and Talented program. He has always been mercurial, energetic, and moody, but until now it was not apparent that his studies were affected. Because his classroom behavior has worsened and his grades have been affected, his fifth grade teacher wanted him evaluated for Attention Deficit Hyperactivity Disorder. Should he be diagnosed with ADHD, what will happen to his gifted and talented status?
   a. Because this has been a documented, ongoing problem, the district will temporarily remove him from the Gifted and Talented program, concentrate on improving his issues with attention and hyperactivity, and then re-enroll him once those things are under control
   b. He will remain in the program and it will be modified to become more appropriate for his learning needs. It is illegal to discriminate against students with learning or behavioral disorders
   c. It will be discussed with the gifted teacher, his general classroom teacher, his parents, and Binh. If Binh promises to monitor his behavior and work to the best of his abilities, he will be permitted to stay
   d. He will be removed from the Gifted and Talented program; his learning issues preclude advanced studies. If, at some future point, he wants to return to the program, he will have to be re-evaluated for it

4. Students identified as gifted and talented can demonstrate serious lack of motivation that hinders their performances. Some of the factors contributing to underachievement are low self-efficacy, not finding the class interesting, not finding the class useful, a student's lack of self-regulation skills, and
  a. When the work is too challenging
  b. If the student is ostracized and unwilling to participate in class
  c. Because the child is so bright, the family has treated him or her with indulgence. As a result, the child expects to be treated as special
  d. The work isn't challenging enough

5. According to Sternberg's triarchic model of intelligence, three central qualities comprise giftedness: componential intelligence (the ability to analyze), experiential intelligence (the ability to think abstractly), and
  a. Creative intelligence
  b. Analytic intelligence
  c. Contextual intelligence
  d. Essential intelligence

6. What type of assessment is often used to identify gifted students in leadership, creativity, or artistic areas?
  a. Qualitative
  b. Quantitative
  c. Both a and b
  d. Formal and informal

7. The steps to curriculum compacting includes understanding learning objectives, identifying students who can master objectives most quickly, pretesting, streamlining instructional periods for students who understand objectives, and:
  a. Recommending acceleration opportunities
  b. Recommending students be advanced a grade
  c. Reviewing assessments
  d. Passing these students on to a Gifted and Talented teacher

8. When creating a Total Talent Portfolio, who is primarily responsible for deciding what to include, maintaining the portfolio, and establishing goals?
  a. The student and the teacher working as partners
  b. The teacher in the primary position, supported by the student
  c. The student in the primary position, with the teacher to review and approve
  d. The student is primarily responsible

9. "Gifted" students are federally defined as:
  a. Those that score above 130 on a WISC test
  b. There is no decisive federal definition; each state determines its own definition
  c. Those who are academically 2 classes or more above peers
  d. Those who exhibit extra-ordinary abilities in the areas of the arts, mathematics, science, e. business, or leadership

10. SAGES stands for:
   a. Standard Assessment Games for English Students, and describes informal assessments based on cooperative games
   b. Sagmore Adams Gates Educational Standards, and describes gifted standards for grades 1-3
   c. Screening Assessment for Gifted Elementary Students, and describes a standardized assessment
   d. Screening Assessment for Gifted Elementary Students, and describes an informal assessment

11. Why are open-ended responses of particular value to the teacher?
   a. The encourage dialogue between teacher and student, or between student and peers
   b. They give the teacher insight into how a particular student structures ideas, uses language, and demonstrates understanding
   c. They are not of particular value because they cannot be measured and do not remain consistent through time
   d. They support the gifted student's emotional and psychological development by demonstrating respect for the student's abilities

12. Self-efficacy, the belief in one's ability to succeed at a particular task, is influenced by past performance, observing the success of peers, verbal support and persuasion by others, and
   a. A willingness to take risks
   b. A creative approach to the task at hand
   c. Strong self-esteem
   d. Physiological cues that indicate nervousness, such as sweating hands; or cues that indicate confidence, such as a feeling of ease and control

13. Ms. Wing often groups her students by ability in order to provide them with efficient, challenging instruction that proceeds at a pace appropriate to their development. She has recently been under attack by some parents, who consider her methods elitist and potentially racist. The parents further point out that so-called 'gifted' students don't need the depth of support that failing students require. The position taken by the National Association of Gifted Children include(s) the following argument(s):
   a. Athletically gifted individuals are regularly grouped by ability and have the best success in such groupings
   b. All areas of professional or graduate study/ preparation involve grouping
   c. Ability grouping is a means by which gifted ELLS, students with economic disadvantages, and those with learning disabilities can be challenged along with their true peers
   d. All of the above

14. Bloom's taxonomy describes the three types of learning as:
   a. Cognitive, affective, and psychomotor
   b. Intellectual, emotional, and social
   c. Intellectual, creative, and psychological
   d. Cognitive, creative, and psychomotor

15. Authentic assessment as it pertains to gifted students:
    a. Assesses emotional development, using expressive models
    b. Assesses learning using portfolios, performance, observations, and other assessments that model real-world representations
    c. Assesses a student's sincerity or authenticity by using a lie-detector
    d. There is no longer such an assessment; popular in the early 1970s, it was abandoned in 1992 because results lacked clarity or concise information

16. Curriculum focusing on social awareness and adjustment, personal awareness and adjustment, a study of attitudes, values, and the individual's perceptions is:
    a. Effective Curriculum
    b. Sociological Curriculum
    c. Affective Curriculum
    d. Developmental Curriculum

17. Mario is taking AP classes at his high school. This means:
    a. Advanced Placement, in which all his high school coursework will also apply as college credits
    b. Alternative Potential. These are small, experimental classes taught to students who have been identified as 'alternative learners'
    c. Accountability Projects. These are independent studies in which an individual or small group works closely with a mentor, who may not be a teacher but someone with professional experience in the student(s) area of interest. Students are held accountable for their projects' designs, implementation, and successful conclusions
    d. Advanced Placement, in which high schools offer coursework meeting criteria recognized by institutions of higher education. Often, college credit is earned when an AP exam in specific content areas is passed

18. Kingore Observation Inventory (KOI) is used to:
    a. The correct name is the Kingmore Ongoing Index; it is used as a continuous informal assessment
    b. Evaluate students in the gifted program to determine if they should remain in the program
    c. Assess the capabilities of English Language Learners with learning disabilities that might be considered for a Gifted and Talented program
    d. Identify gifted and talented students, including those from culturally diverse backgrounds or those who live at or below the poverty level

19. The Elementary and Secondary Education Act signed into law in 2002 is more commonly known as:
    a. The Javits Act
    b. I.D.E.A.
    c. No Child Left Behind
    d. Forward into the Future

20. A number of gifted high school students are in a Language Arts class. Is their AP teacher obliged to differentiate the program of study for the gifted students?
   a. No; if the teacher is already running a student-centered classroom, allowing students choices in assignments, and using flexibility in student grouping, the teacher is already differentiating. No further modification is required
   b. No. All students in Advanced Placement courses are, by definition, gifted. Therefore, differentiation is already taking place
   c. No. The teacher can choose to differentiate the program, but by the time gifted and talented students have entered high school, they have internalized sufficient strategies to challenge themselves and independently promote their own education
   d. Yes. If the teacher is already running a student-centered classroom, allowing choices in assignments, and using flexibility in student grouping, the teacher is already differentiating. The teacher has received additional training to allow him or her to continue to modify classroom assignments to more profoundly challenge the gifted students

21. Mr. Santiago has grouped students with similar interest in architecture and very different learning styles. He has given them a complex project and suggested the initial step to designing the project involves a brief, intense period in which all group members suggest and consider any possible ideas without ranking or judging their value. He reminds them that a flexible mind is capable of taking in more information and making brilliant creative leaps. This creative approach to problem-solving is called:
   a. Brainstorming
   b. Brainraining
   c. Multiple thought process
   d. Creative braining

22. Dr. Acevedo has a gifted child in her fifth grade classroom. In order to keep the student engaged and motivated, which of these inclusion strategies should she permit the student?
   a. Establish own learning goals; self-assess; move to an independent challenge activity when student understands the lesson; encourage student to work with peers close to his or her own intellectual level
   b. Have student independently design his or her own curriculum based upon classroom assignments; self-assess and self-grade; help establish learning goals for the class
   c. Help teacher design his or her own curriculum based upon classroom assignments; review student's assessments and grades with the teacher; suggest learning goals for the class
   d. Help establish learning goals for the class; act as the teacher's assistant teacher; grade work of classmates for the teacher

23. A strategy whereby the curriculum is modified in depth, complexity, and originality, and suggests the four concurrent directions of Core Curriculum, Curriculum of Connections, Curriculum of Practice, and Curriculum of Identity, is called:
   a. Multiple Curriculums Modification
   b. Parallel Curriculum Model
   c. Creative Multiple Curriculums
   d. Parallel Creative Curriculums

24. Gifted and talented teachers are required to have 30 hours of specialized training within the first semester of their teaching, followed by 6 additional hours of training per year. Who determines the material to be covered in this training?
    a. The school board
    b. It is legislated by the state
    c. It is a district decision
    d. It is federally mandated

25. A 4th grade teacher has three gifted students in his general classroom. One strategy for differentiating their learning is extending lessons throughout the curriculum by comparing common themes and issues, studying the associations within and between individual disciplines over the course of time and/or from more than one viewpoint. The teacher is adapting the _____ of his lessons in order to challenge his gifted students.
    a. Complications
    b. Complexity
    c. Enhancement
    d. Richness

26. A middle school teacher has recommended a number of different approaches her students can take with a research project about their hometown. She has suggested students might like to study an aspect of community life (such as social clubs or church organizations) over a significant period of time; compare a variety of architectural styles that are currently found in homes in a certain area; or do a statistical analysis in an area of special interest. One of her students has particular interest in insects. The student has designed a project that tracks insect populations over a thirty-year period in order to understand how draining swampland, cutting trees, and other environmental changes affect such populations. Another student, a painter, is interested in a brief but important art movement that had its roots in the student's hometown. Two students whose parents have recently divorced are designing a project that examines changes the family unit over a century. What teaching strategy is the teacher using?
    a. Continuum of learning experiences
    b. Array of learning experiences
    c. Simultaneous teaching within multiple disciplines
    d. Intellectual freedom of choice

27. The Total Talent model considers which of the following?
    a. Student interest, learning styles, and extraordinary abilities
    b. Student's abilities only
    c. Student's interests and learning styles
    d. A student's interests and learning styles and the student's cognitive ability are equally considered

28. The term 'depth' refers to a number of interconnected strategies employed when exploring an area of study in terms of content. Studying details, patterns, and cultural considerations; examining content from concrete to theoretical; moving from known and familiar to unknown and unfamiliar; and _____ are among these strategies.
    a. Weighing knowledge of the physical world and the spiritual world
    b. Moving beyond theoretical concepts to real-world experience
    c. Considering all previous knowledge and projecting future knowledge
    d. Moving beyond fact to generalizations and principles

29. Eduardo is extremely disorganized. He often fails to turn in work, claiming either that he did turn it in and the teacher lost it, or that it was never assigned. He spends most of his time trying to draw the attention of other 3rd graders through clownish behavior. When that fails, he often falls into depression, claiming that he is worthless. He has been identified as extremely gifted in math, but has fallen behind the rest of the class. What is most likely going on?
    a. He has Attention Deficit Hyperactivity Disorder
    b. He is demonstrating lack of motivation, and may be affected by Attention Deficit Hyperactivity Disorder or a learning disability as well
    c. It is likely he is either indulged or ignored at home and is acting out
    d. He simply lacks self-discipline

30. Eduardo, the student in the above example, was referred for counseling as part of his intervention. Which of the following will the counselor most likely employ?
    a. Help him establish realistic goals for the foreseeable future; focus on his strengths; slowly remediate his weaknesses; do not compare his progress to that of others, but focus on improvements in terms of himself; determine his learning style; build self-esteem through counseling small-group or individual meetings
    b. Establish realistic short and long-term goals for him; focus on his strengths as well as his weaknesses; compare his progress against that of others, but only where the comparison is favorable; determine his learning style; encourage self-esteem through art therapy
    c. Assign realistic short and long-term goals and require he accomplish the steps involved; focus on helping him turn weaknesses into strengths; compare his progress against that of others, honestly and fully; determine his learning style; encourage self-esteem through talk therapy
    d. Assign realistic short and long-term goals and require he document the steps as he follows them; focus him on his weaknesses and assign him the task of developing ways to overcome them; compare his progress against that of others, honestly and fully; determine his learning style; refer him to a psychiatrist who can prescribe medications

31. How many hours of annual training are required of gifted teachers to retain eligibility?
    a. 15
    b. 6
    c. None
    d. 3

32 Who, in addition to gifted and talented teachers, are required to take 6 additional hours of training annually?
    a. Administrators and counselors who make programming or hiring decisions
    b. Only the teachers are required to have annual training
    c. Administrators who make programming or hiring decisions
    d. All teachers, although only gifted and talented teachers are required to have the initial 30 hours of training

33. In determining whether a gifted child is underachieving academically, what should be assessed?
   a. The child's IQ
   b. The child's academic ability
   c. The child's academic performance
   d. The child's psychological development

34. According to Bloom's taxonomy, knowledge, comprehension, application, analysis, synthesis, and evaluation belong to which domain?
   a. Intellectual
   b. Analytical
   c. Cognitive
   d. Mathematical

35. Kaplan has determined that students with which set of beliefs achieve their goals at the highest level?
   a. Belief in self; determination; strong work ethic; willingness to conform
   b. Curiosity; adept at using multiple resources; willing to take risks; applies key words when asking questions
   c. Single-mindedness; determination; belief in self; strong work ethic
   d. Creativity; spontaneity; enthusiasm; joy

36. Students who are gifted are required by federal law to have an Individualized Education Program (IEP).
   a. True. Students in all 50 states receiving any form of special education must have such a plan
   b. False. No such plan for children identified as Gifted and Talented has ever been federally mandated
   c. Neither true nor false. IEPs are used exclusively for students with learning disabilities or mental insufficiencies
   d. At one point this was true, but it has been overturned

37. A student who has tremendous leadership potential has been charged with a series of tasks. She will gather a variety of types of information that describe her areas of strength and continually update this information; she will categorize this material as pertaining to ability, learning styles, social skills, and special interest; she will create a time line to consider options and guide decisions in her differentiation; she will communicate with the teacher regarding these options and decisions; and she will use the information to communicate with mentors, parents, and others about her development. What is she doing?
   a. Creating a Total Talent Portfolio
   b. Developing a number of assessment tools
   c. Developing a differentiation plan
   d. Creating a Personal Growth file

38. Uneven social and intellectual development, being socially at variance with expectations of the classroom and of others at the same age, experiencing finely tuned emotions, and the resulting vulnerability is called:
    a. Social inequality
    b. Psychological ineptitude
    c. Asynchrony
    d. Serendipity

39. Both qualitative and quantitative assessments must be used when identifying elementary, middle, and high school students, with what exception (s)?
    a. Teachers can choose to assess kindergarten students using only qualitative assessments
    b. For students being assessed for exceptional leadership abilities, creativity, or artistic areas, teachers can chose to assess qualitatively only
    c. Both a and b
    d. Neither a nor b

40. Vertical alignment:
    a. Refers to the curriculum-enhancing strategy of stacking lessons into complex groups in order to challenge gifted learners
    b. Means working across the curriculum; various subjects are linked thematically and similar strategies are employed to make learning more relevant
    c. Is seating students according to how well they are achieving academic goals
    d. Refers to mapping the curriculum to build upon understanding and skills learned in the previous grade

41. Differentiation is:
    a. The practice of grouping students in terms of commonality; for example, grouping gifted students and average students separately
    b. Modifying lessons for the unique needs of a particular student
    c. Illegal in all 50 states, as it violates the 14th Amendment
    d. The practice of grouping students in terms of their differences; for example, grouping gifted and regular students, or grouping native English speakers with non-native speakers

42. Gifted and Talented underachievers can best be helped by parents and teacher who _____ in an environment that_____.
    a. Share consistent expectations / is flexible, respects the student's opinions, and does not demand absolute obedience
    b. Demand excellence / is firm, unbending, clear, and consistent
    c. Ask questions / is invigorating, inviting, inspiring, and flexible
    d. Offer support / is loving, understanding, accepting, and respectful

43. Continuum of Learning Experiences refers to:
   a. Challenging experiences and opportunities that resonate with the specific interests and abilities of high-level students
   b. Unplanned learning experiences which are successful and therefore incorporated into the continuum
   c. The correct term is Continuous Learning Events
   d. Planned learning experiences that build upon a progressively stronger foundation from year to year

44. A student who participates in a Gifted and Talented program at her school has been invited to visit family members in China with her parents. She will attend school there, and also be tutored so that she doesn't fall behind. Her mother has asked how a two-month leave of absence will affect her participation in the Gifted and Talented program. Which of the following is most accurate?
   a. If the student takes a leave of absence, she is out of the program
   b. At any point, students will automatically receive furlough status of any length of time as long as the request is in writing six weeks prior to the furlough date
   c. If the student takes a leave of absence, she is out of the program. She can enroll again if the district is willing, but must go through nomination and evaluation procedures
   d. A student may be granted a leave of absence for specific reasons and for a pre-established length of time; the leave must be approved

45. The Total Talent Portfolio is a systematic method of gathering, analyzing, and classifying students' abilities in order to:
   a. Protect gifted children with learning disabilities from falling through the cracks
   b. Help the teacher determine how to enrich and accelerate students' learning based upon their individually unique profiles
   c. Help older students with transition and placement into jobs at which they are likely to excel
   d. Give teachers visual and logistical models whereby they can decide which cross-curriculum strategies are most likely to succeed for individual students

46. Howard Gardner's theory of Multiple Intelligences suggests which categories of intelligences?
   a. Dramatic, musical, verbal, mathematical, dance-oriented, sports-oriented, scientific, and socially concerned
   b. Verbal linguistic, mathematical, musically attuned, visual special, body embraced, interpersonal, naturalistic, and existential
   c. Verbal linguistic, mathematical logical, musical, visual spatial, body kinesthetic, interpersonal, naturalistic, and existential
   d. Emphatic, recessive, aggressive, assertive, dogmatic, apologetic, determined, and elusive

47. A parent has approached his daughter's teacher and is frustrated because the child seems to be completely without motivation. The father has tried rewarding his daughter for exemplary work, punishing her for inadequate work, and reviewing her work before she turns it in to ascertain if it is complete, to no avail. The father knows the daughter is extremely capable intellectually and artistically. He feels both angry at what he sees as her laziness, and guilty for not being able to motivate her. The teacher tells him:
    a. To modify his strategy. He should BOTH reward exemplary work and punish inadequate work at the same time
    b. That until the child takes full responsibility for her actions, no one can motivate her. Withdrawing his involvement will likely result in the girl becoming more motivated
    c. That gifted student's value learning over performance. Her lack of motivation shouldn't be an occasion for blame. Instead of focusing on grades and performance, the father might consider exploring some learning opportunities in areas of the girl's interest. For example, a visit to an art museum followed by a trip to the library for books about a particular art movement might motivate the student
    d. That he is doing all he can do; his methods are fine, and if he changes his course at this point it will do more harm than good

48. The first step in having a student considered for a gifted program is nomination via a Student Observation Form submitted by whom?
    a. Teachers or parents
    b. Other community members
    c. School administrators and other personnel
    d. Any of the above

49. The National Research Center on the Gifted and Talented is:
    a. A federally-funded center with the charter of developing effective methods of identification and testing of Gifted and Talented students, and programming for such students
    b. A federally-funded center with the charter of developing effective methods of showcasing gifted students by funding venues for student performances and presentations
    c. A privately-funded center with the charter of developing effective methods of showcasing gifted students by funding venues for student performances and presentations
    d. A state-funded center with the charter of developing effective methods of identification and testing of Gifted and Talented students, and programming for such students

50. Each school district receives an annual allotment equal to that district's adjusted base allotment multiplied by 0.12 for each student per year. What percentage of students in average daily attendance can be considered for Gifted and Talented funding?
    a. 2.5%
    b. 5%
    c. 10%
    d. 8.3%

51. A district's written policy regarding student identification must: include provisions for continuing screening; include assessment procedures from a number of sources; ensure that all populations have assessment available; ensure final selections are made by at minimum three local educators with specialized training; and:

    a. Include provisions about reassessment, exiting strategies, and readmission policies

    b. Include provisions about furloughs, reassessment, exiting strategies, transferring students, and the district decision appeals process

    c. None of the above; the district is not required to have a written policy

    d. Include provisions about furloughs, reassessment, exiting strategies, transferring students, and parental involvement

52. Luis has been identified as gifted in Mathematics, however, he has been underachieving in that area as well as others for over a year. Shastique is a talented scientist, and has suddenly begun failing most of her classes. She has become withdrawn and easily irritated. Clara, a prima ballerina, is extremely upset that her schoolwork doesn't reflect what she knows she is capable of. Underachievement requires immediate attention:

    a. For Luis and Shastique only; Clara's concern, since her schoolwork is acceptable, is unwarranted

    b. For Shastique only; the suddenness suggests something may have happened at home or elsewhere that must be addressed. Clara is simply being overemotional and Luis appears to be lazy and must learn to motivate himself

    c. For all three students. Underachievement is considered to be a serious problem if it is severe (considerably below grade level), long term, or creating anxiety in the student

    d. For Luis only; his underachievement is clearly long-term

53. In the above example involving Luis, Shastique, and Clara, which set of strategies is most likely to motivate these students?

    a. Extra-credit work to earn bonus grades; put them in leadership positions; and insist upon excellence

    b. Focusing on strengths; let students design their own projects; and differentiated instruction

    c. Therapy; put them in a leadership position for class project which the student designs; and insist upon excellence

    d. Compassionate, authentic dialogue; extra time to complete work; and rubrics which student uses to self-assess

54. Qualitative measures:

    a. Are standardized tests used to assess students

    b. Are assessments that demonstrate to what degree a student's product (artistic or core) demonstrates a high degree of quality

    c. Include all the documents, records, assessments, and products involving a student who is working solely independently, in quarantine

    d. Are anecdotal records, observations, interviews, student products, checklists, and similar materials

55. Bruner, one of the central figures of the 'cognitive revolution,' later became critical of his earlier position and turned his attention to the matter of how _____ shapes thinking.

    a. Creativity

    b. Art

    c. Science

    d. Culture

56. A second-grade teacher has a student who is a very talented artist. The girl has a parent who has asked the teacher how the parent can get involved. Which of the following would be appropriate suggestions for the teacher to make?
   a. Take ongoing notes on her daughter's experiences with the program. Write an evaluation of the program's strengths and weaknesses at the end of the school year
   b. Join the advisory committee to assist in future program planning
   c. Help locate mentorship possibilities and independent study opportunities in the district
   d. All of the above

57. Who is responsible for identifying gifted and talented students?
   a. Each county establishes its own guidelines based upon State Board of Education criteria, which apply to all schools in the county
   b. The State Board of Education is responsible for designing a systematic plan which includes assessment, evaluation, curriculum, and planning. Each district must abide by this overreaching plan, allowing slight modifications when necessary and approved
   c. Each building designs its own system for identifying and serving Gifted and Talented students. It must follow loose guidelines suggested by the district, which in turn, follows loose guidelines suggested by the State
   d. Each district develops and implements a program that is based upon criteria determined by the State Board of Education, which includes identifying and serving gifted and talented students

58. A fourth-grade classroom has four students identified as gifted and talented. There are no special classes in the building. This is a problem because:
   a. All buildings in every district are required to (a) identify gifted and talented students and (b) offer these students differentiated instruction by qualified teachers in pull-out or self-contained classrooms
   b. Any buildings in all districts whose population include identified gifted and talented students are required to offer these students differentiated instruction by qualified teachers in pull-out or self-contained classrooms
   c. This is not a problem, as long as the teacher has obtained 30 hours of professional development and 6 additional hours annually; the gifted students work in groups of three; the gifted students also work independently; and the gifted students have opportunities to work with other students. In addition, the teacher should be able to provide these opportunities to a sufficient degree to challenge the gifted students in addition to serving the remainder of the students
   d. This is not a problem as long as the gifted and talented students are able to receive services through community and professional organizations as well as after-school activities

59. Which is superior in terms of program design accountability, improvement, and development?
   a. A district's promise to guarantee that student assessment and services comply with accountability standards
   b. Continuing formative and summative evaluation strategies that are based on quantitative and qualitative data which is reviewed by the school board
   c. A number of evaluation activities designed to find areas of weakness or inconsistency
   d. Advisement by an organized group consisting of parents, GT students, school staff, and GT staff who meet at regular intervals to study policies and procedures and make recommendations to the district

60. Once a student has been nominated for a gifted and talented program via a Student Observation Form, he or she _____ be assessed.
   a. Will
   b. Might
   c. Will not; nomination guarantees assessment
   d. Must

61. There have been a number of belief systems regarding the nature of intelligence. According to Spearman, intelligence is a measurable cognitive capacity to which a constant number can be assigned; an individual who is intelligent in one area is equally intelligent in others. For Gardner, there are several distinct types of intelligences, and an individual might excel in one area but not another. Sternberg theorizes intelligence is reflected in how successfully an individual handles the changing environment through time. He located cognitive processes in three processes; performance components, knowledge-acquisition components, and:
   a. Metaphoric components
   b. Analytic components
   c. Supercomponents
   d. Metacomponents

62. What is the difference between a raw score and a scale score?
   a. Raw scores are used on specific tests to show how well a student did; this score is not necessarily consistent from test to test. A scale score translates raw scores onto a measurement common to all forms of testing for a particular assessment
   b. There is no difference; both terms refer to the score a student receives
   c. A raw score is shown as an error number while a scale score is indicated by a percentage. For example, if a student takes a test with 100 questions and misses 7, the raw score is -7 and the scale score is 93%.
   d. Scale scores are used on specific tests to show how well a student did; this score is not necessarily consistent from test to test. A raw score translates scale scores onto a measurement common to all forms of testing for a particular assessment

63. Ten year old Ming has exceptional musical abilities. She can hear a piece of music once and immediately play it on a variety of instruments, and her singing range is phenomenal. She is new to the U.S., and speaks little English. She has learning disabilities and is dysgraphic. She is easily excited. Her classmates find her:
    a. Delightful; her excitability coupled with her musical talents are entertaining
    b. Odd; her lack of English, terrible handwriting, nervousness, and bizarre musical talents make her seem abnormal
    c. Acceptable. Fifth graders typically don't exclude one another
    d. Fascinating; her musical talent coupled with her excitability and lack of English make her an interesting distraction to their schoolwork

64. Jasmine, a highly gifted 7th grade student, is picked on by a group of girls. She is mocked for her clothing, which is not fashionable, for her slight stutter, and for her tremendous abilities in Mathematics. The girls call her 'freakish' and 'weird.' Jasmine is deeply hurt by this, and has approached a trusted teacher for advice. What should the teacher suggest?
    a. The teacher should immediately step in, asking to meet with the girls' parents to discuss their daughters' unacceptable behavior.
    b. The teacher should immediately step in, asking to meet with the girls' parents and Jasmine's parents to discuss the unacceptable behavior of the girls who are teasing.
    c. The teacher should speak with the girls individually, informing them that their behavior is unacceptable. Then the teacher should monitor their actions and words toward Jasmine for several weeks to determine if they are still picking on her.
    d. The teacher should talk with Jasmine to help her understand what is most troubling to her. Once Jasmine understands what bothers her and what she would like changed, she should be encouraged to speak with the girls to let them know their behavior is hurtful and that she wants it to stop. If Jasmine requests it, the teacher can also be present to let the girls know this issue is serious, although she should let Jasmine do most of the talking.

65. Parental permission to assess a student for a gifted program is:
    a. Required
    b. Not required, in order to avoid a hardship for students who meets the qualifications but do not have supportive parents
    c. Not required; one of the premises of gifted education is developing a sense of independence and personal responsibility in students
    d. Required only if a student requests parental involvement

66. As described in a study by Dr. Siegle of the Neag Center for Gifted Education, self-efficacy is best defined as:
    a. An individual's belief or feeling about his or her worth to the world or a specific part of it
    b. An individual's belief or feeling about his or her ability regarding a specific undertaking
    c. An individual's belief or feeling about his or her ability to accomplish a goal in an efficient manner
    d. An individual's belief or feeling about how his or her worth will increase if he or she accomplishes a task efficiently and exceptionally well

67. What is the difference between dual and concurrent enrollment?
   a. Concurrent enrollment means being enrolled in a college while still attending high school in order to get college credits. Dual enrollment is enrolling in a college while still in high school in order to get both high school and college credit at the same time
   b. There is no difference; the terms mean the same things
   c. Dual enrollment means being enrolled in a college while still attending high school in order to get college credits. Concurrent enrollment is enrolling in a college while still in high school in order to get both high school and college credit at the same time
   d. The correct term is concurrent enrollment; there is no such thing as dual enrollment

68. Fifth-grade Esmeralda, a gifted writer, told the school counselor that it really isn't her fault that much of her school work never makes it to the teacher's hand. She perceives herself as fairly vulnerable in a difficult world. Her little brother goes through her book bag and tears up her papers. Her handwriting isn't very good no matter how hard she tries and she can't read her own notes. Her mother forces her to stay inside on nice days to do homework that is boring. Sometimes other kids on the bus take her homework and throw it away. Esmeralda is also convinced that when she does manage to turn in the work, the teacher herself misplaces it. She appears to believe her excuses, and doesn't see any way to overcome them. What's going on?
   a. She has a high external locus of control
   b. She has a low external locus of control
   c. She has a low internal locus of control
   d. She has a high internal locus of control

69. Pfeiffer's Gifted Rating Scales is used to:
   a. Weigh the pros and cons of entering a student into a gifted program
   b. Determine what percentage of the budget should be allocated to gifted programs by considering what ratio such program(s) are scaled to
   c. Measure gifted intelligence overall
   d. Measure the degree of disability a gifted, learning-disabled student has

70. A gifted high school student is concerned that her school records might include misinformation. Her parents have requested his records for review. What must the school do?
   a. Obtain written permission directly from the student first
   b. Provide the records within 7 days
   c. Provide the records within 45 days
   d. The school can refuse; by law, they own the records and may share them as they see fit, regardless of requests

71. A differentiation strategy for students with high ability involves streamlining work to match ability, thereby creating a more challenging environment. This is called:
   a. Curriculum packaging
   b. Curriculum packing
   c. Curriculum compacting
   d. Curriculum packeting

72. Gifted students who receive a vertical score equal to or greater than the Met Standard at a grade level higher than their own have already met the standard at their grade level. Is this statement true or false?

    a. True. This is one of the ways gifted students are identified

    b. True, although a student might meet the standard at a higher grade level in one subject but not in all subjects

    c. True. Additionally, gifted students whose vertical score in a particular subject is equal to or greater than the Met Standard at a higher grade level should be working at that higher level, either by taking those classes at that grade level or via differentiation

    d. False

Answers and Explanations

1. D: Have the capability for high accomplishment in intellectual, creative, artistic, or leadership areas or in specific academic fields, and who need services or activities not ordinarily provided by the school to develop those capabilities. The Jacob Javits Gifted and Talented Students Education Act (Javits) is a federal program that addresses the needs of gifted and talented children. The purpose of the Act is to coordinate programs of scientific research, projects, pioneering approaches, and the like to enhance schools' abilities to foster the educational needs of gifted and talented students.

2. B: False. While average and developmentally delayed children typically get very similar scores in a variety of I.Q. tests, gifted children more often get radically differing scores from test to test.

3. B: He will remain in the program and it will be modified to become more appropriate for his learning needs. It is illegal to discriminate against students with learning or behavioral disorders.

4. D: The work isn't challenging enough. Gifted and talented students learn best when they are interested in the material, allowed to explore it independently and are challenged by it. They are not motivated by grades or products so much as by the learning process.

5. C: Contextual intelligence. According to Sternberg's Triarchic Theory of Intelligence, componential intelligence (the ability to analyze, think in abstract terms and efficiently process information), experiential intelligence (the ability to creatively combine unrelated information and to perceive patterns in material that, on the surface, appears to be unrelated) and contextual intelligence (the ability to apply thinking skills to practical situations by reassessing one's position in terms of strengths and weaknesses) are the three core qualities of giftedness.

6. A: Qualitative. While it is appropriate to use both quantitative and qualitative approaches to identify 1st-12th grade students in terms of general intellectual ability or specific academic subjects, a district may choose to apply qualitative assessments only in order to identify gifted students in areas of creativity, the arts and leadership.

7. A: Recommend acceleration opportunities. The steps to curriculum compacting include understanding learning objectives; identify students who can master objectives most quickly, pretest, streamline instructional period for students who understand objectives and recommending acceleration opportunities.

8. D: The student is primarily responsible. One of the purposes of the Total Talent Portfolio is to encourage student autonomy. In taking on responsibility in the selection of materials that will compose the TTP, updating the portfolio at regular intervals and establishing personal goals, the student assumes ownership and is therefore more committed. The teacher's role is that of a guide, primarily in the process of review.

9. B: There is no decisive federal definition; each state determines its own definition. This lack of cohesive classification can be problematic. For example, a child identified as gifted in one state may not be considered so in another. Should the child's family relocate, this could potentially cause a schism that is damaging to the student's equilibrium.

10. C: Screening Assessment for Gifted Elementary Students, and describes a standardized assessment. Unlike many tools used to identify Gifted and Talented students, SAGES was designed expressly for that function. SAGES is also designed to reduce prejudice in gifted and talented testing.

11. B: They give the teacher insight into how a particular student structures ideas, uses language, and demonstrates understanding. Because open-ended questions are the beginning of dialogue, they also give the student the opportunity to express their ideas with creativity, and exhibit the degree of their abilities to abstract, find connections, analyze and assess ideas.

12. D: Physiological cues that indicate nervousness, such as sweating hands; or cues that indicate confidence, such as a feeling of ease and control. Self-efficacy, the belief in one's ability to succeed at a particular task, is influenced by past performance, observing the success of peers, verbal support and persuasion by others, and physiological cues that indicate nervousness, such as sweating hands, or confidence, such as a feeling of ease and control.

13. D: All the above. The National Association of Gifted Children (NAGC) has taken a strong position on grouping. NAGC argues that athletically gifted individuals, whether children or adults, are regularly grouped by ability and have the best success in such groupings. Furthermore, all areas of professional or graduate study/ preparation involve grouping. Yet another argument is that ability grouping is a means by which gifted ELLS, students with economic disadvantages and those with learning disabilities can be challenged along with their true peers.

14. A: Cognitive, affective, and psychomotor. Bloom's taxonomy includes three types of learning. The cognitive has to do with mental skills and is concerned with knowledge. The affective involves feelings and emotions and is concerned with attitude. Psychomotor examines manual/physical facility and is concerned with skills.

15. B: Assesses learning using portfolios, performance, observations, and other assessments that model real-world representations. Authentic assessment tasks are not simply practice for the sake of practice; they are rehearsals for real-world experiences. They assess a wide array of literacy skills in the context of how that skill would be applied in the real world.

16. C: Affective curriculum. Gifted students often feel their differences; they can be more highly attuned to surroundings and non-verbal cues, and they may be reluctant to take risks that would propel them beyond their comfort zones. Affective curriculum allows them the opportunity to explore social and deeply personal aspects of their giftedness.

17. D: Advanced Placement, in which high schools offer coursework meeting criteria recognized by institutions of higher education. Often, college credit is earned when an AP exam in specific content areas is passed.

18. D: Identify gifted and talented students, including those from culturally diverse backgrounds or those who live at or below the poverty level. The Kingore Observation Inventory is an efficient assessment and differentiation process, identifies gifted and talented students via observing behaviors in seven categories.

19. C: No Child Left Behind (NCLB). This legislation reauthorized the Elementary and Secondary Education Act, and allocated financial support for low-income student education, teacher recruitment, professional development, technology and the like. NCLB is aimed at increasing educational success and parental contribution, and charges districts with guaranteeing state proficiency standards in mathematics and reading are reached by 2014.

20. D: Yes. If the teacher is already running a student-centered classroom, allowing choices in assignments and using flexibility in student grouping, she is already differentiating. She has received additional training to allow her to continue to modify classroom assignments to more deeply challenge the gifted students.

21. A: Brainstorming. Brainstorming is a highly-charged creative technique to approach problem-solving, in which group members spontaneously offer a wealth of associations, ideas and possible solutions. The group considers all possibilities without initial judgment, looking for creative possibilities that might otherwise be overlooked.

22. A: Establish own learning goals; self-assess; move to an independent challenge activity when she understands the lesson; encourage her to work with peers close to her intellectual level. Research has proven these techniques more deeply engaged gifted students that traditional methods, and contribute to such students' degree of motivation.

23. B: Parallel Curriculum Model. This strategy modifies the curriculum in depth, complexity and originality and indicates four concurrent directions, Core Curriculum, Curriculum of Connections, Curriculum of Practice and Curriculum of Identity.

24. C: It is a district decision. Prior to assignment in the program, teachers who provide instruction and services for gifted students are required to have a minimum of 30 hours of staff development that includes nature and needs of gifted/talented students, assessing student needs, and curriculum and instruction for gifted students. However, how many hours to devote to each category is left up to the district to determine.

25. B: complexity. Complexity is one strategy for differentiating learning. Extending lessons throughout the curriculum by comparing common themes and issues, studying associations within and between individual disciplines over the course of time and/or from more than one viewpoint are ways a teacher can adapt lessons in order to challenge gifted students.

26. B: Array of learning experiences. An array of learning experiences is defined as a menu of challenging learning experiences or opportunities that fit the unique interests and abilities of advanced level students.

27. D: A student's interests and learning styles and the student's cognitive ability are equally considered. Total Talent Portfolios include attention to student interests and learning styles in addition to cognitive abilities that have traditionally contributed to educational decisions.

28. D: Moving beyond fact to generalizations and principles. Depth involves exploring content within a discipline; analyzing from the concrete to the abstract, familiar to the unfamiliar, known to the unknown; exploring the discipline by going past facts and concepts into generalizations, principles, theories, laws; investigating the layers of experience within a discipline through details, patterns, trends, unanswered questions, ethical considerations.

29. B: He is demonstrating lack of motivation, and may be affected by Attention Deficit Hyperactivity Disorder or a learning disability as well. Many gifted children are not well-organized because they are deeply focused on ideas rather than on the physical world. Many gifted children lack social skills and are either withdrawn or demonstrate attention-seeking behaviors as a result. The cycle spirals downward, often ending in depression. He has been identified as gifted in mathematics, but has fallen behind the rest of his class instead of fulfilling his potential. He is a classically unmotivated gifted student, and might or might not be experiencing a learning disability or ADHD as well.

30. A: Help him establish realistic goals for the foreseeable future; focus on his strengths; slowly remediate his weaknesses; do not compare his progress to that of others, but focus on improvements in terms of himself; determine his learning style; build self-esteem through counseling small-group or individual meetings.

31. B: 6. Teachers working with gifted students are required to complete 30 hours of professional development by the time they finish their first semester, followed by 6 additional hours annually.

32. A: Administrators and counselors who make programming or hiring decisions. All individuals who work with or for children identified as gifted or talented are required to complete 6 hours of training annually.

33. B: The child's academic ability. Gifted children excel in one or more particular areas, but not many can be said to really excel across the board. Examining the gap between what a student is capable of and what that student is actually accomplishing is a good indicator of academic achievement.

34. C: Cognitive. Bloom's taxonomy places knowledge, comprehension, application, analysis, synthesis and evaluation in the cognitive Domain.

35. B: Curiosity; adept at using multiple resources; willing to take risks; applies key words when asking questions. According to Kaplan, belief sets are a strong indicator of learning success. Students who are curious, can move comfortably between resources, are willing to take risks, and listens for key words in questions achieve their goals at the highest level.

36. B: False. No such plan for children identified as gifted and talented has ever been federally mandated. While gifted children do receive special education in terms of differentiation, federal law does not require they have IEPs as learning disabled children are.

37. A: Creating a Total Talent Portfolio. A TTP gathers a variety of types of information describing a student's areas of strength and interest and tracks it through time, updating as appropriate. This information is categorized (typically with a chart) and studied in order to

set goals and determine differentiation. The gifted student is encouraged to develop autonomy by being primarily responsible for her TTP.

38. C: Asynchrony. According to the Columbus Group (1991) "Giftedness is asynchronous development in which advanced cognitive abilities and heightened intensity combine to create inner experiences and awareness that are qualitatively different from the norm. This asynchrony increases with higher intellectual capacity. The uniqueness of the gifted renders them particularly vulnerable and requires modifications in parenting, teaching, and counseling in order for them to develop optimally."

39. C: Both a and b. Many teachers prefer to assess kindergarten students using only qualitative assessments. In areas of creativity, artistic and leadership abilities, teachers can chose to use only qualitative assessments.

40. D: Refers to mapping the curriculum to build upon understanding and skills learned in the previous grade. Vertical curriculum allows teachers to efficiently assess learning from the previous year in order to effectively concentrate time on developing further understanding and skills rather than wasting time with lessons that are redundant in terms of what students already know.

41. B: Differentiate for those students who understand the concept but arrive at incorrect answers. By reviewing their steps, the teacher can determine why answers are incorrect and can demonstrate the correct approach. Concept is more important than content. If the students truly understand the 'how', they have the tools they need to arrive at the 'what'. However, if a student demonstrates the same type of error repeatedly, she may not fully understand the concept. Concept is more important than content.

42. A: Share consistent expectations / is flexible, respects the student's opinions, and does not demand absolute obedience. Gifted underachievers do best when teacher and parent expectations are consistent, and in learning and home environments are not overly rigid or demanding.

43. D: Planned learning experiences that build upon a progressively stronger foundation from year to year. A Continuum of Learning Experiences is a multi-year construct that relies upon each previous year to provide the framework for further academic and artistic development.

44. D: A student may be granted a leave of absence for specific reasons and for a pre-established length of time; the leave must be approved. The leave of absence must all be requested at minimum six weeks prior to the furlough date.

45. B: Help the teacher determine how to enrich and accelerate students' learning based upon their individually unique profiles. The Total Talent Portfolio is a systematic method of gathering, analyzing and classifying students' abilities, given equal weight to interests and learning styles as to cognitive skills to aid the teacher in deciding how to enrich and accelerate students' individualized learning based upon their unique profiles.

46. C: Verbal linguistic, mathematical logical, musical, visual spatial, body kinesthetic, interpersonal, naturalistic, and existential. Gardner's theory of multiple intelligences addresses the nature of intelligence and challenges the accuracy of previous models in

determining degrees of intelligence. His theory is based upon the belief that a person who excels in one area may not show outstanding ability in another, and that all people can be described as exhibiting certain types of intelligence and therefore having differing ways of learning. Bodily kinesthetic learners learn best hands-on. Interpersonal learners learn best when they work within a group. Verbal-linguistic learners are word-oriented, and learn best by reading, writing, and discussing. Logical-mathematical learners base their learning in logic, reason and abstraction. Naturalistic individuals need prior knowledge and experience in order to internalize new information because they recognize and classify in their learning. Visual spatial learners are especially good at mental visualization involving 3 dimensions. Musical learners are sound and rhythm oriented and may learn best when listening to oration, and may use musical phrases as a tool to remembering information.

47. C: That gifted student's value learning over performance. Her lack of motivation shouldn't be an occasion for blame. Instead of focusing on grades and performance, the father might consider exploring some learning opportunities in areas of the girl's interest. For example, a visit to an art museum followed by a trip to the library for books about a particular art movement might motivate the student.

48. D: Any of the above. To be considered for a gifted program, a student must be nominated. Anyone can make the nomination, including family members, teachers, school administrators and other school personnel, and community members who are familiar with the child's abilities.

49. A: A federally-funded center with the charter of developing effective methods of identification and testing of gifted and talented students, and programming for such students. The National Research Center on the Gifted and Talented is one of three components of the Javits Act, a reauthorization of The Elementary and Secondary Education Act.

50. The correct answer is b. 5%. School districts are given an annual allotment equal to a particular district's base allotment multiplied by 12 per student per year. No more than 5% of the total number of students can be considered for Gifted and Talented funding.

51. B: Include provisions about furloughs, reassessment, exiting strategies, transferring students, and the district decision appeals process. A district's written policy regarding student identification must include provisions for continuing screening; assessment procedures from a number of sources; insure that all populations have assessment available; insure final selections are made by at minimum three local educators with specialized training; and contain provisions regarding furloughs or leaves of absence, reassessment, exiting strategies, transferring students and the process by which appeals can be made.

52. C: For all three students. Underachievement is considered to be a serious problem if it is severe (considerably below grade level), long term, or creating anxiety in the student. Although the three students described are involved in different scenarios, all should receive intervention.

53. B: Focusing on strengths; let students design their own projects; and differentiated instruction. As a result of their own sensitivity and peers' sense of them as 'other' or 'strange', many gifted students are vulnerable to insecurities. Focusing on their strengths is

one step in gifted intervention. Gifted students are also highly motivated by their individual interests; allowing them to design their own projects can engage them at a level classroom work does not. Differentiated instruction is essential to the education of gifted and talented students; curriculum compacting, proper pacing and deepening the lesson are all ways in which differentiation can be useful.

54. D: Are anecdotal records, observations, interviews, student products, checklists, and similar materials. In contrast, quantitative measures involve standardized testing.

55. D: Culture. Bruner's original position on education underwent a major shift by the mid 1990s. In The Culture of Education he expresses the position that it is impossible to think outside of culture; regardless of how interior or 'mental' the process, thinking requires the framework or grid of culture.

56. D: All of the above. Parental involvement is an important piece in successful education. The teacher could suggest the mother take ongoing notes on her daughter's experiences with the gifted program; give her evaluation of the program's strengths and weaknesses at the end of the school year; join the advisory committee to assist in future program planning; and help locate mentorship possibilities and independent study opportunities in the district.

57. D: Each district develops and implements a program that is based upon criteria determined by the State Board of Education, which includes identifying and serving gifted and talented students.

58. C: This is not a problem, as long as the teacher has obtained 30 hours of professional development and 6 additional hours annually; the gifted students work in groups of three; the gifted students also work independently; and the gifted students have opportunities to work with other students. In addition, the teacher should be able to provide these opportunities to a sufficient degree to challenge the gifted students in addition to serving the remainder of the students.

59. B: Continuing formative and summative evaluation strategies that are based on quantitative and qualitative data which is reviewed by the school board. This provides superior accountability over a district's promise to guarantee student assessment and services comply with accountability standards; multiple evaluations to locate areas of weakness; or advisement by a group of parents, students, and school staff who study policies and procedures and make recommendations to the district.

60. B: Might. The decision of whether to assess a child is made by a committee and is partially based on observable academic strength according. If the G/T Committee decides a particular child should be assessed, parents must first give permission.

61. D: Metacomponents. Sternberg theorizes intelligence is reflected in how successfully an individual handles the changing environment through time. He located cognitive processes in three processes; performance components, knowledge-acquisition components and metacomponents. Metacomponents are self-aware processes that contribute to making decisions and solving problems; they can be seen as instances of the mind being aware of the mind.

62. A: Raw scores are used on specific tests to show how well a student did; this score is not necessarily consistent from test to test. A scale score translates raw scores onto a measurement common to all forms of testing for a particular assessment.

63. The correct response is b: Odd; her lack of English, terrible handwriting, nervousness, and bizarre musical talents make her seem abnormal. Many gifted children are highly sensitive and can be far more easily excited that their average peers. They may not know how to relate to other children, and as a result lack social skills. Ming's lack of English, terrible handwriting, nervousness and musical talents might make her seem abnormal to her classmates.

64. D: The teacher should talk with Jasmine to help her understand what is most troubling to her. Once Jasmine understands what bothers her and what she would like changed, she should be encouraged to speak with the girls to let them know their behavior is hurtful and that she wants it to stop. If Jasmine requests it, the teacher can also be present to let the girls know this issue is serious, although she should let Jasmine do most of the talking.

65. A: Required. Unless the student has been emancipated, a parent or guardian must give written permission before that student can participate in a Gifted and Talented program.

66. B: An individual's belief or feeling about his or her ability regarding a specific undertaking. An unmotivated gifted student may have low self-efficacy, believing that a task, project or other undertaking is beyond his abilities.

67. A: Concurrent enrollment means being enrolled in a college while still attending high school in order to get college credits. Dual enrollment is enrolling in a college while still in high school in order to get both high school and college credit at the same time.

68. A: She has a high external locus of control. Locus of control is the degree to which an individual believes she can control events or actions that impact them. The more in control an individual believes herself to be, the higher her internal locus of control. The less in control an individual believes herself to be, the higher her external locus of control. In this example, the student blames other students, her brother and her teacher for missing schoolwork, believing herself to have no control in these matters. Her locus of control is external, and the degree to which she feels out of control indicates it is also high.

69. A: Weigh the pros and cons of entering a student into a gifted program. Pfeiffer's Scales is a time-efficient way to assess giftedness using six scales for students beyond kindergarten. It is administered by teachers and covers intellectual ability, academic ability, creativity, artistic talent, leadership ability, and motivation.

70. C: Provide the records within 45 days. The Family Educational Rights and Privacy Act (FERPA), is a federal law that addresses student rights regarding their records. Among FERPA regulations is the requirement that a student be given records within 45 days of request.

71. C: Curriculum compacting. Curriculum compacting is a differentiation strategy for students with high ability involves streamlining work to match ability, thereby creating a more challenging environment. The three steps to compacting are determining goals, identifying students, and offering acceleration and enrichment opportunities. Curriculum

compacting eliminates repetition of lessons that have already been learned, and speeding up lessons to match the learner's pace.

72. D: False. Vertical scores at a particular grade level indicate the degree of mastery of that subject at that grade level. This number is unrelated to the Standards established at a higher grade level. Vertical scores are not the same as Standards.

Secret Key #1 - Time is Your Greatest Enemy

Pace Yourself

Wear a watch. At the beginning of the test, check the time (or start a chronometer on your watch to count the minutes), and check the time after every few questions to make sure you are "on schedule."

If you are forced to speed up, do it efficiently. Usually one or more answer choices can be eliminated without too much difficulty. Above all, don't panic. Don't speed up and just begin guessing at random choices. By pacing yourself, and continually monitoring your progress against your watch, you will always know exactly how far ahead or behind you are with your available time. If you find that you are one minute behind on the test, don't skip one question without spending any time on it, just to catch back up. Take 15 fewer seconds on the next four questions, and after four questions you'll have caught back up. Once you catch back up, you can continue working each problem at your normal pace.

Furthermore, don't dwell on the problems that you were rushed on. If a problem was taking up too much time and you made a hurried guess, it must be difficult. The difficult questions are the ones you are most likely to miss anyway, so it isn't a big loss. It is better to end with more time than you need than to run out of time.

Lastly, sometimes it is beneficial to slow down if you are constantly getting ahead of time. You are always more likely to catch a careless mistake by working more slowly than quickly, and among very high-scoring test takers (those who are likely to have lots of time left over), careless errors affect the score more than mastery of material.

Secret Key #2 - Guessing is not Guesswork

You probably know that guessing is a good idea - unlike other standardized tests, there is no penalty for getting a wrong answer. Even if you have no idea about a question, you still have a 20-25% chance of getting it right.

Most test takers do not understand the impact that proper guessing can have on their score. Unless you score extremely high, guessing will significantly contribute to your final score.

Monkeys Take the Test

What most test takers don't realize is that to insure that 20-25% chance, you have to guess randomly. If you put 20 monkeys in a room to take this test, assuming they answered once per question and behaved themselves, on average they would get 20-25% of the questions correct. Put 20 test takers in the room, and the average will be much lower among guessed questions. Why?
1. The test writers intentionally write deceptive answer choices that "look" right. A test taker has no idea about a question, so picks the "best looking" answer, which is often wrong. The monkey has no idea what looks good and what doesn't, so will consistently be lucky about 20-25% of the time.
2. Test takers will eliminate answer choices from the guessing pool based on a hunch or intuition.

Simple but correct answers often get excluded, leaving a 0% chance of being correct. The monkey has no clue, and often gets lucky with the best choice.

This is why the process of elimination endorsed by most test courses is flawed and detrimental to your performance- test takers don't guess, they make an ignorant stab in the dark that is usually worse than random.

$5 Challenge

Let me introduce one of the most valuable ideas of this course- the $5 challenge:

You only mark your "best guess" if you are willing to bet $5 on it.
You only eliminate choices from guessing if you are willing to bet $5 on it.

Why $5? Five dollars is an amount of money that is small yet not insignificant, and can really add up fast (20 questions could cost you $100). Likewise, each answer choice on one question of the test will have a small impact on your overall score, but it can really add up to a lot of points in the end.

The process of elimination IS valuable. The following shows your chance of guessing it right:

If you eliminate wrong answer choices until only this many remain:	Chance of getting it correct:
1	100%
2	50%
3	33%

However, if you accidentally eliminate the right answer or go on a hunch for an incorrect answer, your chances drop dramatically: to 0%. By guessing among all the answer choices, you are

GUARANTEED to have a shot at the right answer.

That's why the $5 test is so valuable- if you give up the advantage and safety of a pure guess, it had better be worth the risk.

What we still haven't covered is how to be sure that whatever guess you make is truly random. Here's the easiest way:

Always pick the first answer choice among those remaining.

Such a technique means that you have decided, **before you see a single test question**, exactly how you are going to guess- and since the order of choices tells you nothing about which one is correct, this guessing technique is perfectly random.

This section is not meant to scare you away from making educated guesses or eliminating choices- you just need to define when a choice is worth eliminating. The $5 test, along with a pre-defined random guessing strategy, is the best way to make sure you reap all of the benefits of guessing.

Secret Key #3 - Practice Smarter, Not Harder

Many test takers delay the test preparation process because they dread the awful amounts of practice time they think necessary to succeed on the test. We have refined an effective method that will take you only a fraction of the time.

There are a number of "obstacles" in your way to succeed. Among these are answering questions, finishing in time, and mastering test-taking strategies. All must be executed on the day of the test at peak performance, or your score will suffer. The test is a mental marathon that has a large impact on your future. Just like a marathon runner, it is important to work your way up to the full challenge. So first you just worry about questions, and then time, and finally strategy:

Success Strategy

1. Find a good source for practice tests.
2. If you are willing to make a larger time investment, consider using more than one study guide- often the different approaches of multiple authors will help you "get" difficult concepts.
3. Take a practice test with no time constraints, with all study helps "open book." Take your time with questions and focus on applying strategies.
4. Take a practice test with time constraints, with all guides "open book."
5. Take a final practice test with no open material and time limits

If you have time to take more practice tests, just repeat step 5. By gradually exposing yourself to the full rigors of the test environment, you will condition your mind to the stress of test day and maximize your success.

Secret Key #4 - Prepare, Don't Procrastinate

Let me state an obvious fact: if you take the test three times, you will get three different scores. This is due to the way you feel on test day, the level of preparedness you have, and, despite the test writers' claims to the contrary, some tests WILL be easier for you than others.

Since your future depends so much on your score, you should maximize your chances of success. In order to maximize the likelihood of success, you've got to prepare in advance. This means taking practice tests and spending time learning the information and test taking strategies you will need to succeed.

Never take the test as a "practice" test, expecting that you can just take it again if you need to. Feel free to take sample tests on your own, but when you go to take the official test, be prepared, be focused, and do your best the first time!

Secret Key #5 - Test Yourself

Everyone knows that time is money. There is no need to spend too much of your time or too little of your time preparing for the test. You should only spend as much of your precious time preparing as is necessary for you to get the score you need.

Once you have taken a practice test under real conditions of time constraints, then you will know if you are ready for the test or not.

If you have scored extremely high the first time that you take the practice test, then there is not much point in spending countless hours studying. You are already there.

Benchmark your abilities by retaking practice tests and seeing how much you have improved. Once you score high enough to guarantee success, then you are ready.

If you have scored well below where you

need, then knuckle down and begin studying in earnest. Check your improvement regularly through the use of practice tests under real conditions. Above all, don't worry, panic, or give up. The key is perseverance!

Then, when you go to take the test, remain confident and remember how well you did on the practice tests. If you can score high enough on a practice test, then you can do the same on the real thing.

General Strategies

The most important thing you can do is to ignore your fears and jump into the test immediately- do not be overwhelmed by any strange-sounding terms. You have to jump into the test like jumping into a pool- all at once is the easiest way.

Make Predictions
As you read and understand the question, try to guess what the answer will be. Remember that several of the answer choices are wrong, and once you begin reading them, your mind will immediately become cluttered with answer choices designed to throw you off. Your mind is typically the most focused immediately after you have read the question and digested its contents. If you can, try to predict what the correct answer will be. You may be surprised at what you can predict.

Quickly scan the choices and see if your prediction is in the listed answer choices. If it is, then you can be quite confident that you have the right answer. It still won't hurt to check the other answer choices, but most of the time, you've got it!

Answer the Question
It may seem obvious to only pick answer choices that answer the question, but the test writers can create some excellent answer choices that are wrong. Don't pick an answer just because it sounds right, or you believe it to be true. It MUST answer the question. Once you've made your selection, always go back and check it against the question and make sure that you didn't misread the question, and the answer choice does answer the question posed.

Benchmark
After you read the first answer choice, decide if you think it sounds correct or not. If it doesn't, move on to the next answer choice. If it does, mentally mark that answer choice. This doesn't mean that you've definitely selected it as your answer choice, it just means that it's the best you've seen thus far. Go ahead and read the next choice. If the next choice is worse than the one you've already selected, keep going to the next answer choice. If the next choice is better than the choice you've already selected, mentally mark the new answer choice as your best guess.

The first answer choice that you select becomes your standard. Every other answer choice must be benchmarked against that standard. That choice is correct until proven otherwise by another answer choice beating it out. Once you've decided that no other answer choice seems as good, do one final check to ensure that your answer choice answers the question posed.

Valid Information
Don't discount any of the information provided in the question. Every piece of information may be necessary to determine the correct answer. None of the information in the question is there to throw you off (while the answer choices will certainly have information to throw you off). If two seemingly unrelated topics are discussed, don't ignore either. You can be confident there is a

relationship, or it wouldn't be included in the question, and you are probably going to have to determine what is that relationship to find the answer.

Avoid "Fact Traps"

Don't get distracted by a choice that is factually true. Your search is for the answer that answers the question. Stay focused and don't fall for an answer that is true but incorrect. Always go back to the question and make sure you're choosing an answer that actually answers the question and is not just a true statement. An answer can be factually correct, but it MUST answer the question asked. Additionally, two answers can both be seemingly correct, so be sure to read all of the answer choices, and make sure that you get the one that BEST answers the question.

Milk the Question

Some of the questions may throw you completely off. They might deal with a subject you have not been exposed to, or one that you haven't reviewed in years. While your lack of knowledge about the subject will be a hindrance, the question itself can give you many clues that will help you find the correct answer. Read the question carefully and look for clues. Watch particularly for adjectives and nouns describing difficult terms or words that you don't recognize. Regardless of if you completely understand a word or not, replacing it with a synonym either provided or one you more familiar with may help you to understand what the questions are asking. Rather than wracking your mind about specific detailed information concerning a difficult term or word, try to use mental substitutes that are easier to understand.

The Trap of Familiarity

Don't just choose a word because you recognize it. On difficult questions, you may not recognize a number of words in the answer choices. The test writers don't put "make-believe" words on the test; so don't think that just because you only recognize all the words in one answer choice means that answer choice must be correct. If you only recognize words in one answer choice, then focus on that one. Is it correct? Try your best to determine if it is correct. If it is, that is great, but if it doesn't, eliminate it. Each word and answer choice you eliminate increases your chances of getting the question correct, even if you then have to guess among the unfamiliar choices.

Eliminate Answers

Eliminate choices as soon as you realize they are wrong. But be careful! Make sure you consider all of the possible answer choices. Just because one appears right, doesn't mean that the next one won't be even better! The test writers will usually put more than one good answer choice for every question, so read all of them. Don't worry if you are stuck between two that seem right. By getting down to just two remaining possible choices, your odds are now 50/50. Rather than wasting too much time, play the odds. You are guessing, but guessing wisely, because you've been able to knock out some of the answer choices that you know are wrong. If you are eliminating choices and realize that the last answer choice you are left with is also obviously wrong, don't panic. Start over and consider each choice again. There may easily be something that you missed the first time and will realize on the second pass.

Tough Questions

If you are stumped on a problem or it appears too hard or too difficult, don't waste time. Move on! Remember though, if you can quickly check for obviously incorrect answer choices, your chances of guessing correctly are greatly improved. Before you completely give up, at least try to knock out a couple of possible answers. Eliminate what you can and then guess at the remaining answer choices before moving on.

Brainstorm

If you get stuck on a difficult question, spend a few seconds quickly brainstorming. Run through the complete list of possible answer choices. Look at each choice and ask yourself, "Could this answer the question satisfactorily?" Go through each answer choice and consider it independently of the other. By systematically going through all possibilities, you may find something that you would otherwise overlook. Remember that when you get stuck, it's important to try to keep moving.

Read Carefully

Understand the problem. Read the question and answer choices carefully. Don't miss the question because you misread the terms. You have plenty of time to read each question thoroughly and make sure you understand what is being asked. Yet a happy medium must be attained, so don't waste too much time. You must read carefully, but efficiently.

Face Value

When in doubt, use common sense. Always accept the situation in the problem at face value. Don't read too much into it. These problems will not require you to make huge leaps of logic. The test writers aren't trying to throw you off with a cheap trick. If you have to go beyond creativity and make a leap of logic in order to have an answer choice answer the question, then you should look at the other answer choices. Don't overcomplicate the problem by creating theoretical relationships or explanations that will warp time or space. These are normal problems rooted in reality. It's just that the applicable relationship or explanation may not be readily apparent and you have to figure things out. Use your common sense to interpret anything that isn't clear.

Prefixes

If you're having trouble with a word in the question or answer choices, try dissecting it. Take advantage of every clue that the word might include. Prefixes and suffixes can be a huge help. Usually they allow you to determine a basic meaning. Pre- means before, post- means after, pro - is positive, de- is negative. From these prefixes and suffixes, you can get an idea of the general meaning of the word and try to put it into context. Beware though of any traps. Just because con is the opposite of pro, doesn't necessarily mean congress is the opposite of progress!

Hedge Phrases

Watch out for critical "hedge" phrases, such as likely, may, can, will often, sometimes, often, almost, mostly, usually, generally, rarely, sometimes. Question writers insert these hedge phrases to cover every possibility. Often an answer choice will be wrong simply because it leaves no room for exception. Avoid answer choices that have definitive words like "exactly," and "always".

Switchback Words

Stay alert for "switchbacks". These are the words and phrases frequently used to alert you to shifts in thought. The most common switchback word is "but". Others include although, however, nevertheless, on the other hand, even though, while, in spite of, despite, regardless of.

New Information

Correct answer choices will rarely have completely new information included. Answer choices typically are straightforward reflections of the material asked about and will directly relate to the question. If a new piece of information is included in an answer choice that doesn't even seem to relate to the topic being asked about, then that answer choice is likely incorrect. All of

- 133 -

the information needed to answer the question is usually provided for you, and so you should not have to make guesses that are unsupported or choose answer choices that require unknown information that cannot be reasoned on its own.

Time Management

On technical questions, don't get lost on the technical terms. Don't spend too much time on any one question. If you don't know what a term means, then since you don't have a dictionary, odds are you aren't going to get much further. You should immediately recognize terms as whether or not you know them. If you don't, work with the other clues that you have, the other answer choices and terms provided, but don't waste too much time trying to figure out a difficult term.

Contextual Clues

Look for contextual clues. An answer can be right but not correct. The contextual clues will help you find the answer that is most right and is correct. Understand the context in which a phrase or statement is made. This will help you make important distinctions.

Don't Panic

Panicking will not answer any questions for you. Therefore, it isn't helpful. When you first see the question, if your mind goes blank, take a deep breath. Force yourself to mechanically go through the steps of solving the problem and using the strategies you've learned.

Pace Yourself

Don't get clock fever. It's easy to be overwhelmed when you're looking at a page full of questions, your mind is full of random thoughts and feeling confused, and the clock is ticking down faster than you would like. Calm down and maintain the pace that you have set for yourself. As long as you are on track by monitoring your pace, you are guaranteed to have

enough time for yourself. When you get to the last few minutes of the test, it may seem like you won't have enough time left, but if you only have as many questions as you should have left at that point, then you're right on track!

Answer Selection

The best way to pick an answer choice is to eliminate all of those that are wrong, until only one is left and confirm that is the correct answer. Sometimes though, an answer choice may immediately look right. Be careful! Take a second to make sure that the other choices are not equally obvious. Don't make a hasty mistake. There are only two times that you should stop before checking other answers. First is when you are positive that the answer choice you have selected is correct. Second is when time is almost out and you have to make a quick guess!

Check Your Work

Since you will probably not know every term listed and the answer to every question, it is important that you get credit for the ones that you do know. Don't miss any questions through careless mistakes. If at all possible, try to take a second to look back over your answer selection and make sure you've selected the correct answer choice and haven't made a costly careless mistake (such as marking an answer choice that you didn't mean to mark). This quick double check should more than pay for itself in caught mistakes for the time it costs.

Beware of Directly Quoted Answers

Sometimes an answer choice will repeat word for word a portion of the question or reference section. However, beware of such exact duplication – it may be a trap! More than likely, the correct choice will paraphrase or summarize a point, rather than being exactly the same wording.

Slang

Scientific sounding answers are better than slang ones. An answer choice that begins "To compare the outcomes..." is much more likely to be correct than one that begins "Because some people insisted..."

Extreme Statements

Avoid wild answers that throw out highly controversial ideas that are proclaimed as established fact. An answer choice that states the "process should be used in certain situations, if..." is much more likely to be correct than one that states the "process should be discontinued completely." The first is a calm rational statement and doesn't even make a definitive, uncompromising stance, using a hedge word "if" to provide wiggle room, whereas the second choice is a radical idea and far more extreme.

Answer Choice Families

When you have two or more answer choices that are direct opposites or parallels, one of them is usually the correct answer. For instance, if one answer choice states "x increases" and another answer choice states "x decreases" or "y increases," then those two or three answer choices are very similar in construction and fall into the same family of answer choices. A family of answer choices is when two or three answer choices are very similar in construction, and yet often have a directly opposite meaning. Usually the correct answer choice will be in that family of answer choices. The "odd man out" or answer choice that doesn't seem to fit the parallel construction of the other answer choices is more likely to be incorrect.

Special Report: What Your Test Score Will Tell You About Your IQ

Did you know that most standardized tests correlate very strongly with IQ? In fact, your general intelligence is a better predictor of your success than any other factor, and most tests intentionally measure this trait to some degree to ensure that those selected by the test are truly qualified for the test's purposes.

Before we can delve into the relation between your test score and IQ, I will first have to explain what exactly is IQ. Here's the formula:

Your IQ = 100 + (Number of standard deviations below or above the average)*15

Now, let's define standard deviations by using an example. If we have 5 people with 5 different heights, then first we calculate the average. Let's say the average was 65 inches. The standard deviation is the "average distance" away from the average of each of the members. It is a direct measure of variability - if the 5 people included Jackie Chan and Shaquille O'Neal, obviously there's a lot more variability in that group than a group of 5 sisters who are all within 6 inches in height of each other. The standard deviation uses a number to characterize the average range of difference within a group.

A convenient feature of most groups is that they have a "normal" distribution- makes sense that most things would be normal, right? Without getting into a bunch of statistical mumbo-jumbo, you just need to know that if you know the average of the group and the standard deviation, you can successfully predict someone's percentile rank in the group.

Confused? Let me give you an example. If instead of 5 people's heights, we had 100 people, we could figure out their rank in height JUST by knowing the average, standard deviation, and their height. We wouldn't need to know each person's height and manually rank them, we could just predict their rank based on three numbers.

What this means is that you can take your PERCENTILE rank that is often given with your test and relate this to your RELATIVE IQ of people taking the test - that is, your IQ relative to the people taking the test. Obviously, there's no way to know your actual IQ because the people taking a standardized test are usually not very good samples of the general population- many of those with extremely low IQ's never achieve a level of success or competency necessary to complete a typical standardized test. In fact, professional psychologists who measure IQ actually have to use non-written tests that can fairly measure the IQ of those not able to complete a traditional test.

The bottom line is to not take your test score too seriously, but it is fun to compute your "relative IQ" among the people who took the test with you. I've done the calculations below. Just look up your percentile rank in the left and then you'll see your "relative IQ" for your test in the right hand column-

Percentile Rank	Your Relative IQ		Percentile Rank	Your Relative IQ
99	135		59	103
98	131		58	103
97	128		57	103
96	126		56	102
95	125		55	102
94	123		54	102
93	122		53	101
92	121		52	101
91	120		51	100
90	119		50	100
89	118		49	100
88	118		48	99
87	117		47	99
86	116		46	98
85	116		45	98
84	115		44	98
83	114		43	97
82	114		42	97
81	113		41	97
80	113		40	96
79	112		39	96
78	112		38	95
77	111		37	95
76	111		36	95
75	110		35	94
74	110		34	94
73	109		33	93
72	109		32	93
71	108		31	93
70	108		30	92
69	107		29	92
68	107		28	91
67	107		27	91
66	106		26	90
65	106		25	90
64	105		24	89
63	105		23	89
62	105		22	88
61	104		21	88
60	104		20	87

Special Report: What is Test Anxiety and How to Overcome It?

The very nature of tests caters to some level of anxiety, nervousness or tension, just as we feel for any important event that occurs in our lives. A little bit of anxiety or nervousness can be a good thing. It helps us with motivation, and makes achievement just that much sweeter. However, too much anxiety can be a problem; especially if it hinders our ability to function and perform.

"Test anxiety," is the term that refers to the emotional reactions that some test-takers experience when faced with a test or exam. Having a fear of testing and exams is based upon a rational fear, since the test-taker's performance can shape the course of an academic career. Nevertheless, experiencing excessive fear of examinations will only interfere with the test-takers ability to perform, and his/her chances to be successful.

There are a large variety of causes that can contribute to the development and sensation of test anxiety. These include, but are not limited to lack of performance and worrying about issues surrounding the test.

Lack of Preparation

Lack of preparation can be identified by the following behaviors or situations:

Not scheduling enough time to study, and therefore cramming the night before the test or exam
Managing time poorly, to create the sensation that there is not enough time to do everything
Failing to organize the text information in advance, so that the study material consists of the entire text and not simply the pertinent information
Poor overall studying habits

Worrying, on the other hand, can be related to both the test taker, or many other factors around him/her that will be affected by the results of the test. These include worrying about:

Previous performances on similar exams, or exams in general
How friends and other students are achieving
The negative consequences that will result from a poor grade or failure

There are three primary elements to test anxiety. Physical components, which involve the same typical bodily reactions as those to acute anxiety (to be discussed below). Emotional factors have to do with fear or panic. Mental or cognitive issues concerning attention spans and memory abilities.

Physical Signals

There are many different symptoms of test anxiety, and these are not limited to mental and emotional strain. Frequently there are a range of physical signals that will let a test taker know that he/she is suffering from test anxiety. These bodily changes can include the following:

Perspiring
Sweaty palms
Wet, trembling hands
Nausea
Dry mouth
A knot in the stomach
Headache
Faintness
Muscle tension
Aching shoulders, back and neck
Rapid heart beat
Feeling too hot/cold

To recognize the sensation of test anxiety, a test-taker should monitor him/herself for the following sensations:

The physical distress symptoms as listed above
Emotional sensitivity, expressing emotional feelings such as the need to cry or laugh too much, or a sensation of anger or helplessness
A decreased ability to think, causing the test-taker to blank out or have racing thoughts that are hard to organize or control.

Though most students will feel some level of anxiety when faced with a test or exam, the majority can cope with that anxiety and maintain it at a manageable level. However, those who cannot are faced with a very real and very serious condition, which can and should be controlled for the immeasurable benefit of this sufferer.

Naturally, these sensations lead to negative results for the testing experience. The most common effects of test anxiety have to do with nervousness and mental blocking.

Nervousness

Nervousness can appear in several different levels:

The test-taker's difficulty, or even inability to read and understand the questions on the test
The difficulty or inability to organize thoughts to a coherent form
The difficulty or inability to recall key words and concepts relating to the testing questions (especially essays)
The receipt of poor grades on a test, though the test material was well known by the test taker

Conversely, a person may also experience mental blocking, which involves:

Blanking out on test questions
Only remembering the correct answers to the questions when the test has already finished.

Fortunately for test anxiety sufferers, beating these feelings, to a large degree, has to do with proper preparation. When a test taker has a feeling of preparedness, then anxiety will be dramatically lessened.

The first step to resolving anxiety issues is to distinguish which of the two types of anxiety are being suffered. If the anxiety is a direct result of a lack of preparation, this should be considered a normal reaction, and the anxiety level (as opposed to the test results) shouldn't be anything to worry about. However, if, when adequately prepared, the test-taker still panics, blanks out, or seems to overreact, this is not a fully rational reaction. While this can be considered normal too, there are many ways to combat and overcome these effects.

Remember that anxiety cannot be entirely eliminated, however, there are ways to minimize it, to make the anxiety easier to manage. Preparation is one of the best ways to minimize test anxiety. Therefore the following techniques are wise in order to best fight off any anxiety that may want to build.

To begin with, try to avoid cramming before a test, whenever it is possible. By trying to memorize an entire term's worth of information in one day, you'll be shocking your system, and not giving yourself a very good chance to absorb the information. This is an easy path to anxiety, so for those who suffer from test anxiety, cramming should not even be considered an option.

Instead of cramming, work throughout the semester to combine all of the material which is presented throughout the semester, and work on it gradually as the course goes by, making sure to master the main concepts first, leaving minor details for a week or so before the test.

To study for the upcoming exam, be sure to pose questions that may be on the examination, to gauge the ability to answer them by integrating the ideas from your texts, notes and lectures, as well as any supplementary readings.

If it is truly impossible to cover all of the information that was covered in that particular term, concentrate on the most important portions, that can be covered very well. Learn these concepts as best as possible, so that when the test comes, a goal can be made to use these concepts as presentations of your knowledge.

In addition to study habits, changes in attitude are critical to beating a struggle with test anxiety. In fact, an improvement of the perspective over the entire test-taking experience can actually help a test taker to enjoy studying and therefore improve the overall experience. Be certain not to overemphasize the significance of the grade - know that the result of the test is neither a reflection of self worth, nor is it a measure of intelligence; one grade will not predict a person's future success.

- 140 -

To improve an overall testing outlook, the following steps should be tried:

Keeping in mind that the most reasonable expectation for taking a test is to expect to try to demonstrate as much of what you know as you possibly can.
Reminding ourselves that a test is only one test; this is not the only one, and there will be others.
The thought of thinking of oneself in an irrational, all-or-nothing term should be avoided at all costs.
A reward should be designated for after the test, so there's something to look forward to. Whether it be going to a movie, going out to eat, or simply visiting friends, schedule it in advance, and do it no matter what result is expected on the exam.

Test-takers should also keep in mind that the basics are some of the most important things, even beyond anti-anxiety techniques and studying. Never neglect the basic social, emotional and biological needs, in order to try to absorb information. In order to best achieve, these three factors must be held as just as important as the studying itself.

Study Steps

Remember the following important steps for studying:

Maintain healthy nutrition and exercise habits. Continue both your recreational activities and social pass times. These both contribute to your physical and emotional well being.
Be certain to get a good amount of sleep, especially the night before the test, because when you're overtired you are not able to perform to the best of your best ability.
Keep the studying pace to a moderate level by taking breaks when they are needed, and varying the work whenever possible, to keep the mind fresh instead of getting bored. When enough studying has been done that all the material that can be learned has been learned, and the test taker is prepared for the test, stop studying and do something relaxing such as listening to music, watching a movie, or taking a warm bubble bath.

There are also many other techniques to minimize the uneasiness or apprehension that is experienced along with test anxiety before, during, or even after the examination. In fact, there are a great deal of things that can be done to stop anxiety from interfering with lifestyle and performance. Again, remember that anxiety will not be eliminated entirely, and it shouldn't be. Otherwise that "up" feeling for exams would not exist, and most of us depend on that sensation to perform better than usual. However, this anxiety has to be at a level that is manageable.

Of course, as we have just discussed, being prepared for the exam is half the battle right away. Attending all classes, finding out what knowledge will be expected on the exam, and knowing the exam schedules are easy steps to lowering anxiety. Keeping up with work will remove the need to cram, and efficient study habits will eliminate wasted time. Studying should be done in an ideal location for concentration, so that it is simple to become interested in the material and give it complete attention. A method such as SQ3R (Survey, Question, Read, Recite, Review) is a wonderful key to follow to make sure that the study habits are as effective as possible, especially in the case of learning from a textbook. Flashcards are great techniques for memorization. Learning to take good notes will mean that notes will be full of useful information, so that less sifting will need to be done to seek out what is pertinent for studying. Reviewing notes after class and then again on occasion will keep the information fresh in the mind. From notes that have been taken summary sheets and outlines can be made for simpler reviewing.

A study group can also be a very motivational and helpful place to study, as there will be a sharing of ideas, all of the minds can work together, to make sure that everyone understands, and the studying will be made more interesting because it will be a social occasion.

Basically, though, as long as the test-taker remains organized and self confident, with efficient study habits, less time will need to be spent studying, and higher grades will be achieved.

To become self confident, there are many useful steps. The first of these is "self talk." It has been shown through extensive research, that self-talk for students who suffer from test anxiety, should be well monitored, in order to make sure that it contributes to self confidence as opposed to sinking the student. Frequently the self talk of test-anxious students is negative or self-defeating, thinking that everyone else is smarter and faster, that they always mess up, and that if they don't do well, they'll fail the entire course. It is important to decreasing anxiety that awareness is made of self talk. Try writing any negative self thoughts and then disputing them with a positive statement instead. Begin self-encouragement as though it was a friend speaking. Repeat positive statements to help reprogram the mind to believing in successes instead of failures.

Helpful Techniques

Other extremely helpful techniques include:

Self-visualization of doing well and reaching goals
While aiming for an "A" level of understanding, don't try to "overprotect" by setting your expectations lower. This will only convince the mind to stop studying in order to meet the lower expectations.
Don't make comparisons with the results or habits of other students. These are individual factors, and different things work for different people, causing different results.
Strive to become an expert in learning what works well, and what can be done in order to improve. Consider collecting this data in a journal.
Create rewards for after studying instead of doing things before studying that will only turn into avoidance behaviors.
Make a practice of relaxing - by using methods such as progressive relaxation, self-hypnosis, guided imagery, etc - in order to make relaxation an automatic sensation.
Work on creating a state of relaxed concentration so that concentrating will take on the focus of the mind, so that none will be wasted on worrying.
Take good care of the physical self by eating well and getting enough sleep.
Plan in time for exercise and stick to this plan.

Beyond these techniques, there are other methods to be used before, during and after the test that will help the test-taker perform well in addition to overcoming anxiety.

Before the exam comes the academic preparation. This involves establishing a study schedule and beginning at least one week before the actual date of the test. By doing this, the anxiety of not having enough time to study for the test will be automatically eliminated. Moreover, this will make the studying a much more effective experience, ensuring that the learning will be an easier process. This relieves much undue pressure on the test-taker.

Summary sheets, note cards, and flash cards with the main concepts and examples of these main concepts should be prepared in advance of the actual studying time. A topic should never be eliminated from this process. By omitting a topic because it isn't expected to be on the test is only setting up the test-taker for anxiety should it actually appear on the exam. Utilize the course syllabus for laying out the topics that should be studied. Carefully go over the notes that were made in class, paying special attention to any of the issues that the professor took special care to emphasize while lecturing in class. In the textbooks, use the chapter review, or if possible, the chapter tests, to begin your review.

It may even be possible to ask the instructor what information will be covered on the exam, or what the format of the exam will be (for example, multiple choice, essay, free form, true-false). Additionally, see if it is possible to find out how many questions will be on the test. If a review sheet or sample test has been offered by the professor, make good use of it, above anything else, for the preparation for the test. Another great resource for getting to know the examination is reviewing tests from previous semesters. Use these tests to review, and aim to achieve a 100% score on each of the possible topics. With a few exceptions, the goal that you set for yourself is the highest one that you will reach.

Take all of the questions that were assigned as homework, and rework them to any other possible course material. The more problems reworked, the more skill and confidence will form as a result. When forming the solution to a problem, write out each of the steps. Don't simply do head work. By doing as many steps on paper as possible, much clarification and therefore confidence will be formed. Do this with as many homework problems as possible, before checking the answers. By checking the answer after each problem, a reinforcement will exist, that will not be on the exam. Study situations should be as exam-like as possible, to prime the test-taker's system for the experience. By waiting to check the answers at the end, a psychological advantage will be formed, to decrease the stress factor.

Another fantastic reason for not cramming is the avoidance of confusion in concepts, especially when it comes to mathematics. 8-10 hours of study will become one hundred percent more effective if it is spread out over a week or at least several days, instead of doing it all in one sitting. Recognize that the human brain requires time in order to assimilate new material, so frequent breaks and a span of study time over several days will be much more beneficial.

Additionally, don't study right up until the point of the exam. Studying should stop a minimum of one hour before the exam begins. This allows the brain to rest and put things in their proper order. This will also provide the time to become as relaxed as possible when going into the examination room. The test-taker will also have time to eat well and eat sensibly. Know that the brain needs food as much as the rest of the body. With enough food and enough sleep, as well as a relaxed attitude, the body and the mind are primed for success.

Avoid any anxious classmates who are talking about the exam. These students only spread anxiety, and are not worth sharing the anxious sentimentalities.

Before the test also involves creating a positive attitude, so mental preparation should also be a point of concentration. There are many keys to creating a positive attitude. Should fears become rushing in, make a visualization of taking the exam, doing well, and seeing an A written on the paper. Write out a list of affirmations that will bring a feeling of confidence, such as "I am doing well in my English class," "I studied well and know my material," "I enjoy this class." Even if the affirmations aren't believed at first, it sends a positive message to the subconscious which will result in an alteration of the overall belief system, which is the system that creates reality.

If a sensation of panic begins, work with the fear and imagine the very worst! Work through the entire scenario of not passing the test, failing the entire course, and dropping out of school, followed by not getting a job, and pushing a shopping cart through the dark alley where you'll live. This will place things into perspective! Then, practice deep breathing and create a visualization of the opposite situation - achieving an "A" on the exam, passing the entire course, receiving the degree at a graduation ceremony.

On the day of the test, there are many things to be done to ensure the best results, as well as the most calm outlook. The following stages are suggested in order to maximize test-taking potential:

Begin the examination day with a moderate breakfast, and avoid any coffee or beverages with caffeine if the test taker is prone to jitters. Even people who are used to managing caffeine can feel jittery or light-headed when it is taken on a test day. Attempt to do something that is relaxing before the examination begins. As last minute cramming clouds the mastering of overall concepts, it is better to use this time to create a calming outlook.
Be certain to arrive at the test location well in advance, in order to provide time to select a location that is away from doors, windows and other distractions, as well as giving enough time to relax before the test begins.
Keep away from anxiety generating classmates who will upset the sensation of stability and relaxation that is being attempted before the exam.
Should the waiting period before the exam begins cause anxiety, create a self-distraction by reading a light magazine or something else that is relaxing and simple.

During the exam itself, read the entire exam from beginning to end, and find out how much time should be allotted to each individual problem. Once writing the exam, should more time be taken for a problem, it should be abandoned, in order to begin another problem. If there is time at the end, the unfinished problem can always be returned to and completed.

Read the instructions very carefully - twice - so that unpleasant surprises won't follow during or after the exam has ended.

When writing the exam, pretend that the situation is actually simply the completion of homework within a library, or at home. This will assist in forming a relaxed atmosphere, and will allow the brain extra focus for the complex thinking function.

Begin the exam with all of the questions with which the most confidence is felt. This will build the confidence level regarding the entire exam and will begin a quality momentum. This will also create encouragement for trying the problems where uncertainty resides.

Going with the "gut instinct" is always the way to go when solving a problem. Second guessing should be avoided at all costs. Have confidence in the ability to do well.

For essay questions, create an outline in advance that will keep the mind organized and make certain that all of the points are remembered. For multiple choice, read every answer, even if the correct one has been spotted - a better one may exist.

Continue at a pace that is reasonable and not rushed, in order to be able to work carefully. Provide enough time to go over the answers at the end, to check for small errors that can be corrected.

Should a feeling of panic begin, breathe deeply, and think of the feeling of the body releasing sand through its pores. Visualize a calm, peaceful place, and include all of the sights, sounds and sensations of this image. Continue the deep breathing, and take a few minutes to continue this with closed eyes. When all is well again, return to the test.

If a "blanking" occurs for a certain question, skip it and move on to the next question. There will be time to return to the other question later. Get everything done that can be done, first, to guarantee all the grades that can be compiled, and to build all of the confidence possible. Then return to the weaker questions to build the marks from there.

Remember, one's own reality can be created, so as long as the belief is there, success will follow. And remember: anxiety can happen later, right now, there's an exam to be written!

After the examination is complete, whether there is a feeling for a good grade or a bad grade, don't dwell on the exam, and be certain to follow through on the reward that was promised...and enjoy it! Don't dwell on any mistakes that have been made, as there is nothing that can be done at this point anyway.

Additionally, don't begin to study for the next test right away. Do something relaxing for a while, and let the mind relax and prepare itself to begin absorbing information again.

From the results of the exam - both the grade and the entire experience, be certain to learn from what has gone on. Perfect studying habits and work some more on confidence in order to make the next examination experience even better than the last one.

Learn to avoid places where openings occurred for laziness, procrastination and day dreaming.

Use the time between this exam and the next one to better learn to relax, even learning to relax on cue, so that any anxiety can be controlled during the next exam. Learn how to relax the body. Slouch in your chair if that helps. Tighten and then relax all of the different muscle groups, one group at a time, beginning with the feet and then working all the way up to the neck and face. This will ultimately relax the muscles more than they were to begin with. Learn how to breath deeply and comfortably, and focus on this breathing going in and out as a relaxing thought. With every exhale, repeat the word "relax."

As common as test anxiety is, it is very possible to overcome it. Make yourself one of the test-takers who overcome this frustrating hindrance.

Special Report: Retaking the Test: What Are Your Chances at Improving Your Score?

After going through the experience of taking a major test, many test takers feel that once is enough. The test usually comes during a period of transition in the test taker's life, and taking the test is only one of a series of important events. With so many distractions and conflicting recommendations, it may be difficult for a test taker to rationally determine whether or not he should retake the test after viewing his scores.

The importance of the test usually only adds to the burden of the retake decision. However, don't be swayed by emotion. There a few simple questions that you can ask yourself to guide you as you try to determine whether a retake would improve your score:

1. What went wrong? Why wasn't your score what you expected?

Can you point to a single factor or problem that you feel caused the low score? Were you sick on test day? Was there an emotional upheaval in your life that caused a distraction? Were you late for the test or not able to use the full time allotment? If you can point to any of these specific, individual problems, then a retake should definitely be considered.

2. Is there enough time to improve?

Many problems that may show up in your score report may take a lot of time for improvement. A deficiency in a particular math skill may require weeks or months of tutoring and studying to improve. If you have enough time to improve an identified weakness, then a retake should definitely be considered.

3. How will additional scores be used? Will a score average, highest score, or most recent score be used?

Different test scores may be handled completely differently. If you've taken the test multiple times, sometimes your highest score is used, sometimes your average score is computed and used, and sometimes your most recent score is used. Make sure you understand what method will be used to evaluate your scores, and use that to help you determine whether a retake should be considered.

4. Are my practice test scores significantly higher than my actual test score?

If you have taken a lot of practice tests and are consistently scoring at a much higher level than your actual test score, then you should consider a retake. However, if you've taken five practice tests and only one of your scores was higher than your actual test score, or if your practice test scores were only slightly higher than your actual test score, then it is unlikely that you will significantly increase your score.

5. Do I need perfect scores or will I be able to live with this score? Will this score still allow me to follow my dreams?

What kind of score is acceptable to you? Is your current score "good enough?" Do you have to have a certain score in order to pursue the future of your dreams? If you won't be happy with your current score, and there's no way that you could live with it, then you should consider a retake. However, don't get your hopes up. If you are looking for significant improvement, that may or may not be possible. But if you won't be happy otherwise, it is at least worth the effort.
Remember that there are other considerations. To achieve your dream, it is likely that your grades may also be taken into account. A great test score is usually not the only thing necessary to succeed. Make sure that you aren't overemphasizing the importance of a high test score.

Furthermore, a retake does not always result in a higher score. Some test takers will score lower on a retake, rather than higher. One study shows that one-fourth of test takers will achieve a significant improvement in test score, while one-sixth of test takers will actually show a decrease. While this shows that most test takers will improve, the majority will only improve their scores a little and a retake may not be worth the test taker's effort.

Finally, if a test is taken only once and is considered in the added context of good grades on the part of a test taker, the person reviewing the grades and scores may be tempted to assume that the test taker just had a bad day while taking the test, and may discount the low test score in favor of the high grades. But if the test is retaken and the scores are approximately the same, then the validity of the low scores are only confirmed. Therefore, a retake could actually hurt a test taker by definitely bracketing a test taker's score ability to a limited range.

Special Report: Additional Bonus Material

Due to our efforts to try to keep this book to a manageable length, we've created a link that will give you access to all of your additional bonus material.

Please visit http://www.mometrix.com/bonus948/placegt to access the information.